Raspberry Pi Hardware Reference

Warren W. Gay

Apress®

Raspberry Pi Hardware Reference

ISBN-13 (pbk): 978-1-4842-0800-7

ISBN-13 (electronic): 978-1-4842-0799-4

Managing Director: Welmoed Spahr
Lead Editor: Michelle Lowman
Development Editor: Douglas Pundick
Technical Reviewer: Stewart Watkiss
Editorial Board: Steve Anglin, Mark Beckner, Ewan Buckingham, Gary Cornell, Louise Corrigan, Jim DeWolf, Jonathan Gennick, Robert Hutchinson, Michelle Lowman, James Markham, Matthew Moodie, Jeff Olson, Jeffrey Pepper, Douglas Pundick, Ben Renow-Clarke, Dominic Shakeshaft, Gwenan Spearing, Matt Wade, Steve Weiss
Coordinating Editor: Kevin Walter
Copy Editors: Sharon Wilkey and Kim Wimpsett
Compositor: SPi Global
Indexer: SPi Global
Artist: SPi Global
Cover Designer: Anna Ishchenko

Distributed to the book trade worldwide by Springer Science+Business Media New York, 233 Spring Street, 6th Floor, New York, NY 10013. Phone 1-800-SPRINGER, fax (201) 348-4505, e-mail orders-ny@springer-sbm.com, or visit www.springeronline.com. Apress Media, LLC is a California LLC and the sole member (owner) is Springer Science + Business Media Finance Inc (SSBM Finance Inc). SSBM Finance Inc is a **Delaware** corporation.

For information on translations, please e-mail rights@apress.com, or visit www.apress.com.

Apress and friends of ED books may be purchased in bulk for academic, corporate, or promotional use. eBook versions and licenses are also available for most titles. For more information, reference our Special Bulk Sales–eBook Licensing web page at www.apress.com/bulk-sales.

Any source code or other supplementary material referenced by the author in this text is available to readers at www.apress.com. For detailed information about how to locate your book's source code, go to www.apress.com/source-code/.

This book is dedicated to the memory of my father, Charles Wallace Gay, who passed away this year. He didn't remember it when we discussed it last, but he was responsible for sparking my interest in electronics at an early age. He had brought home from his used-car business two D cells, a piece of blue automotive wire, and a flashlight bulb. After showing me how to hold them together to complete the circuit and light the bulb, I was hooked for life.

I am also indebted to my family for their patience, particularly my wife Jacqueline, who tries to understand why I need to do the things I do with wires, solder, and parts arriving in the mail. I am glad for even grudging acceptance because I'm not sure that I could give up the thrill of moving electrons in some new way. Sometimes hobby electronics projects have no real justification beyond "because we can!"

Contents at a Glance

Contents

About the Author

Warren W. Gay started out in electronics at an early age, dragging discarded TVs and radios home from public school. In high school he developed a fascination for programming the IBM 1130 computer, which resulted in a career plan change to software development. After attending Ryerson Polytechnical Institute, he has enjoyed a software developer career for more than 30 years, programming mainly in C/C++. Warren has been programming Linux since 1994 as an open source contributor and professionally on various Unix platforms since 1987.

Before attending Ryerson, Warren built an Intel 8008 system from scratch before there were CP/M systems and before computers got personal. In later years, Warren earned an advanced amateur radio license (call sign VE3WWG) and worked the amateur radio satellites. A high point of his ham radio hobby was making digital contact with the Mir space station (U2MIR) in 1991.

Warren works at Datablocks.net, an enterprise-class ad-serving software services company. There he programs C++ server solutions on Linux back-end systems.

About the Technical Reviewer

 **Stewart Watkiss** graduated from the University of Hull, United Kingdom, with a master's degree in electronic engineering. He has been a fan of Linux since first installing it on a home computer during the late 1990s. While working as a Linux system administrator, he was awarded Advanced Linux Certification (LPIC 2) in 2006 and created the Penguin Tutor website to help others learning Linux and working toward Linux certification (www.penguintutor.com).

Stewart is a big fan of the Raspberry Pi. He owns several Raspberry Pi computers that he uses to help to protect his home (Internet filter), provide entertainment (XBMC), and teach programming to his two children. He also volunteers as a STEM ambassador, going into local schools to help support teachers and teach programming to teachers and children.

Acknowledgments

In the making of a book, there are so many people involved. I first want to thank Michelle Lowman, acquisitions editor, for her enthusiasm for the initial manuscript and pulling this project together. Enthusiasm goes a long way in an undertaking like this.

I'd also like to thank Kevin Walter, coordinating editor, for handling all my email questions and correspondence and coordinating things. I greatly appreciated the technical review performed by Stewart Watkiss, checking the facts presented, the formulas, the circuits, and the software. Independent review produces a much better end product.

Thanks also to Sharon Wilkey for patiently wading through the copy edit for me. Judging from the amount of editing, I left her plenty to do. Thanks to Douglas Pundick, development editor, for his oversight and believing in this book. Finally, my thanks to all the other unseen people at Apress who worked behind the scenes to bring this text to print.

I would be remiss if I didn't thank my friends for helping me with the initial manuscript. My guitar teacher, Mark Steiger, and my brother-in-law's brother, Erwin Bendiks, both volunteered their time to help me with the first manuscript. Mark has no programming or electronics background and probably deserves an award for reading through "all that stuff." I am indebted also to my daughter, Laura, and her husband, Michael Burton, for taking the time to take my photograph while planning their wedding at that time.

There are so many others I could list who helped me along the way. To all of you, please accept my humble thanks, and may God bless.

Introduction

After receiving your first Raspberry Pi, the first question in your mind is probably "What can this hardware do?" What are its capabilities and limitations? Hardware is the more urgent question because software is so easily altered or replaced.

The one perplexing problem I immediately ran up against when I started out with the Pi was that the hardware information seemed to be scattered. The basic information was accessible and well known, but other important parameters such as GPIO source or sink current limits required research. After researching these questions, I often discovered that the answer was "It depends." It was the answering of these classes of questions that led to the writing of *Mastering the Raspberry Pi*.

Content of This Book

This book is focused mainly on the Raspberry Pi's hardware. The content is extracted from the complete work, *Mastering the Raspberry Pi*. As such, it will serve you as an owner's manual of sorts, saving time as a ready reference about the hardware you purchased.

While this is a volume focused on hardware, some software coverage must coexist. For example, it is through the physical memory management that software gains access to the hardware peripheral registers. Another example is the discussion about the CPU, where the pthread API is covered for reference purposes. Through the application of this API, you further utilize that ARM CPU.

This book begins by introducing the Pi in general terms in Chapter 1. Then attention immediately turns to the important topic of power in Chapter 2. Many people suffer needless problems because of neglect in this area. The chapter ends with some notes about running from battery or solar power.

Chapter 3 documents the header strips, LEDs, and Reset inputs. This is information that should be bookmarked. Next is Chapter 4 on memory, which documents the various Raspbian Linux measures and controls for memory allocation. The CPU and its API are described in Chapter 5.

The focus of Chapter 6 is USB. USB-specific power issues and its API are explained. Wired and wireless Ethernet networking is discussed in Chapter 7. SD card technology is examined in Chapter 8, describing the interface and the specifics of the Raspberry Pi interface. The topic of wear leveling is also included.

Serial communication, RS-232 converters, serial consoles, and dedicated serial ports are covered in Chapter 9. The serial interface, some historical influences, and flow control are discussed. Included is an organized description of the Linux API for utilizing the serial interface.

Chapter 10 covers the important area of the GPIO interface. Every aspect of GPIO is covered, including its configuration after reset and boot. Logic levels, drive strength, input pullup resistor control, and output totem pole configuration are explained. Each is examined from an electronics viewpoint. Additionally, the various ways of applying these GPIO pins in software are described.

The GPIO coverage also includes guidance about how to budget the +3.3 V supply current. Configuration of the pins and selection of alternate I/O functions are also discussed. Finally, a design procedure is provided for a single transistor driver, when more power is required.

The next three chapters concern themselves with Raspbian Linux–supported peripheral buses. The one-wire driver is supported through a Linux driver and described in Chapter 11. The I2C bus is another important peripheral bus, which is documented with its API in Chapter 12. Finally, the SPI bus is explained with its API in Chapter 13. With this coverage, you will be fully informed of what is available and how to leverage Raspbian Linux to drive it.

Assumptions About You

Apart from the C language software API presented in this book, much of the content of this volume is electronics based. You should therefore have a basic understanding of digital electronics. This includes a good grasp of DC voltage, current, resistance, power, and mastery of Ohm's law (you may also refer to Appendix C). For a full appreciation of the concepts behind the I2C bus, you should also be familiar with the operation of an open collector driver.

The transistor driver design procedure provided in Chapter 10 (GPIO) uses a *light* engineering approach where formulas are *assumed* (an engineering text would also include the *derivation* of the formulas). The intent here is to simply demonstrate that the use of design procedure can solve problems that might otherwise cause students to look for a *chip* solution when a *transistor* would suffice. Let's take the fear out of design.

Learn and Design

The main assumption throughout this book is that you are looking to learn how to design things for yourself. Through an appreciation of the involved hardware parameters, design procedure, and the software API, you will be able to build custom solutions using the Raspberry Pi. To further assist in this, several charts and tables were provided in this reference. Any real designer takes delight in having the necessary parameters available at their disposal.

CHAPTER 1

■ ■ ■

The Raspberry Pi

Before considering the details about each resource within the Raspberry Pi, it is useful to take a high-level inventory. In this chapter, let's just list what you get when you purchase a Pi.

In later chapters, you'll be looking at each resource from two perspectives:

- The hardware itself—what it is and how it works

- The driving software and API behind it

In some cases, the hardware will have one or more kernel modules behind it, forming the device driver layer. They expose a software API that interfaces between the application and the hardware device. For example, applications communicate with the driver by using ioctl(2) calls, while the driver communicates with the I2C devices on the bus. The /sys/class file system is another way that device drivers expose themselves to applications. You'll see this when you examine GPIO in Chapter 10.

There are some cases where drivers don't currently exist in Raspbian Linux. An example is the Pi's PWM peripheral that is covered in Chapter 9 of *Experimenting with Raspberry Pi* (Apress, 2014). Here we must map the device's registers into the application memory space and drive the peripheral directly from the application. Both direct access and driver access have their advantages and disadvantages.

So while our summary inventory here simply lists the hardware devices, you'll be examining each from a hardware and software point of view in the chapters ahead.

Models

A hardware inventory is directly affected by the model of the unit being examined. The Raspberry Pi comes in two models:

- Model A (introduced later as a hardware-reduced model)

- Model B (introduced first and is the full hardware model)

Figure 1-1 shows the Model B and its interfaces. Table 1-1 indicates the differences between the two models.

***Figure 1-1.** Model B interfaces*

***Table 1-1.** Model Differences*

Resource	Model A	Model B
RAM	256 MB	512 MB
USB ports	1	2
Ethernet port	None	10/100 Ethernet (RJ45)
Power consumption[10]	300 mA (1.5 W)	700 mA (3.5 W)
Target price[9]	$25.00	$35.00

As you can see, one of the first differences to note is the amount of RAM available. The revision 2.0 (Rev 2.0) Model B has 512 MB of RAM instead of 256 MB. The GPU also shares use of the RAM. So keep that in mind when budgeting RAM.

In addition, the Model A does not include an Ethernet port but can support networking through a USB network adapter. Keep in mind that only one USB port exists on the Model A, requiring a hub if other USB devices are needed.

Finally, the power consumption differs considerably between the two models. The Model A is listed as requiring 300 mA vs. 700 mA for the Model B. Both of these figures should be considered low because consumption rises considerably when the GPU is active (when using the desktop through the HDMI display port).

The maximum current flow that is permitted through the 5 V micro-USB connection is about 1.1 A because of the fuse. However, when purchasing a power supply/adapter, it is recommended that you seek supplies that are rated higher than 1.2 A because they often don't live up to their specifications. Chapter 2 provides more details about power supplies.

Hardware in Common

The two Raspberry Pi models share some common features, which are summarized in Table 1-2.[9] The Hardware column lists the broad categories; the Features column provides additional specifics.

Table 1-2. Common Hardware Features

Hardware*	Features	Comments
System on a chip	Broadcom BCM2835	CPU, GPU, DSP, SDRAM, and USB port
CPU model Clock rate	ARM1176JZF-S core	With floating point
	700 MHz	Overclockable to 800 MHz
GPU	Broadcom VideoCore IV	
	OpenGL ES 2.0	3D
	OpenVG	3D
	MPEG-2	
	VC-1	Microsoft, licensed
	1080p30 H.264	Blu-ray Disc capable, 40 Mbit/s
	MPEG-4	AVC high-profile decoder and encoder
	1 Gpixel/s, 1.5 Gtexels/s	24 GFLOPS with DMA
Video output	Composite RCA	PAL and NTSC
	HDMI	Rev 1.3 and 1.4
	Raw LCD panels	Via DSI
Audio output	3.5 mm jack HDMI	

(continued)

Table 1-2. *(continued)*

Hardware	Features	Comments
Storage	SD/MMC/SDIO	Card slot
Peripherals	8 × GPIO	
	UART	
	I2C bus	100 kHz
	SPI bus	Two chip selects, +3.3 V, +5 V, ground
Power source	5 V via micro-USB	

Which Model?

One of the questions that naturally follows a model feature comparison is why the Model A? Why wouldn't everyone just buy Model B?

Power consumption is one deciding factor. If your application is battery powered, perhaps a data-gathering node in a remote location, then power consumption becomes a critical factor. If the unit is supplemented by solar power, the Model A's power requirements are more easily satisfied.

Cost is another advantage. When an Arduino/AVR class of application is being considered, the added capability of the Pi running Linux, complete with a file system on SD, makes it irresistible. Especially at the model A price of $25.

Unit cost may be critical to students in developing countries. Networking can be sacrificed, if it still permits the student to learn on the cheaper Model A. If network capability is needed later, even temporarily, a USB network adapter can be attached or borrowed.

The main advantage of the Model B is its networking capability. Networking today is so often taken for granted. Yet it remains a powerful way to integrate a larger system of components. The project outlined in Chapter 8 of *Experimenting with Raspberry Pi* (Apress, 2014) demonstrates how powerful ØMQ (ZeroMQ) can be in bringing separate nodes together.

■ ■ ■

## CHAPTER 2

Power

One of the most frequently neglected parts of a system tends to be the power supply—at least when everything is working. Only when things get weird does the power supply begin to get some scrutiny.

The Raspberry Pi owner needs to give the power supply extra respect. Unlike many AVR class boards, where the raw input voltage is followed by an onboard 5 V regulator, the Pi expects its power to be regulated at the input. The Pi does include onboard regulators, but these regulate to lower voltages (3.3 V and lower).

Figure 2-1 illustrates the rather fragile Micro-USB power input connector. There is a large round capacitor directly behind the connector that people often grab for leverage. It is a mistake to grab it, however, as many have reported "popping it off" by accident.

Figure 2-1. *Micro-USB power input*

Calculating Power

Sometimes power supplies are specified in terms of voltage, and power handling capability in watts. The Pi's input voltage of 5 V must support a *minimum* of 700 mA (Model B). Let's compute a power supply figure in watts (this does not include any added peripherals):

$$P = V \times I$$
$$= 5 \times 0.7$$
$$= 3.5 \text{ W}$$

The 3.5 W represents a minimum requirement, so we should overprovision this by an additional 50%:

$$P = 3.5 \times 1.50$$
$$= 5.25 \text{ W}$$

The additional 50% yields a power requirement of 5.25 W.

■ **Tip** Allow 50% extra capacity for your power supply. A power supply gone bad may cause damage or many other problems. One common power-related problem for the Pi is loss of data on the SD card.

Current Requirement

Since the power supply being sought produces one output voltage (5 V), you'll likely see adapters with advertised *current* ratings instead of power. In this case, you can simply factor a 50% additional current instead:

$$I_{supply} = I_{Pi} \times 1.50$$
$$= 0.700 \times 1.50$$
$$= 1.05 \text{ A}$$

To double-check our work, let's see whether this agrees with the power rating we computed earlier:

$$P = V \times I$$
$$= 5 \times 1.05$$
$$= 5.25 \text{ W}$$

The result does agree. You can conclude this section knowing that you *minimally* need a 5 V supply that produces one of the following:

- 5.25 W or more

- 1.05 A or more (ignoring peripherals)

Supplies that can meet either requirement, should be sufficient. However, you should be aware that not all advertised ratings are what they seem. Cheap supplies often fail to meet their own claims, so an additional margin must always be factored in.

Peripheral Power

Each additional circuit that draws power, especially USB peripherals, must be considered in a power budget. Depending on its type, a given USB peripheral plugged into a USB 2 port can expect up to 500 mA of current, assuming it can obtain it. (Pre Rev 2.0 USB ports were limited to 140 mA by polyfuses.)

Wireless adapters are known to be power hungry. Don't forget about the keyboard and mouse when used, since they also add to the power consumption. If you've attached an RS-232 level shifter circuit (perhaps using MAX232CPE), you should budget for that small amount also in the 3 V supply budget. This will indirectly add to your +5 V budget, since the 3 V regulator is powered from it. (The USB ports use the +5 V supply.) Anything that draws power from your Raspberry Pi should be tallied.

Model B Input Power

The Raspberry Pi's input voltage is fixed at exactly 5 V (±0.25 V). Looking at the schematic in Figure 2-2, you can see how the power enters the micro-USB port on the pin marked VBUS. Notice that the power flows through fuse F3, which is rated at 6 V, 1.1 A. If after an accidental short, you find that you can't get the unit to power up, check that fuse with an ohmmeter.

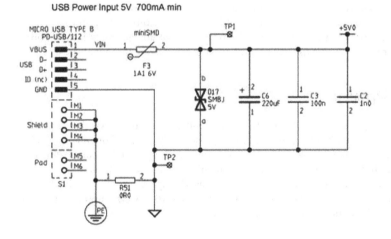

Figure 2-2. *Model B Rev 2.0 input power*

If you bring the input +5 V power into the Pi through header P1, P5, or TP1, for example, you will lose the safety of the fuse F3. So if you bypass the micro-USB port to bring in power, you may want to include a safety fuse in the supplying circuit.

Figure 2-3 shows the 3.3 V regulator for the Pi. Everything at the 3.3 V level is supplied by this regulator, and the current is limited by it.

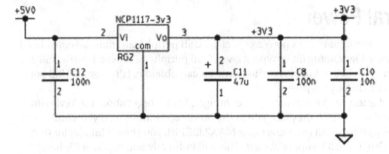

Figure 2-3. *3.3 V power*

Model A Input Power

Like the Model B, the Model A receives its power from the micro-USB port. The Model A power requirement is 300 mA, which is easily supported by a powered USB hub or desktop USB 2 port. A USB 2 port is typically able to supply a maximum of 500 mA unless the power is divided among neighboring ports. You may find in practice, however, that not all USB ports will deliver 500 mA.

As with the Model B, factor the power required by your USB peripherals. If your total nears or exceeds 500 mA, you may need to power your Model A from a separate power source. Don't try to run a wireless USB adapter from the Model A's USB port if the Pi is powered by a USB port itself. The total current needed by the Pi and wireless adapter will likely exceed 500 mA. Supply the wireless adapter power from a USB hub, or power the Pi from a 1.2 A or better power source. Also be aware that not all USB hubs function correctly under Linux, so check compatibility if you're buying one for that purpose.

3.3 Volt Power

Since the 3.3 V supply appears at P1-01, P1-17, and P5-02, it is useful to examine Figure 2-3 (shown previously) to note its source. This supply is indirectly derived from the input 5 V supply, passing through regulator RG2. The maximum excess current that can be drawn from it is 50 mA; the Raspberry Pi uses up the remaining capacity of this regulator.

When planning a design, you need to budget this 3 V supply carefully. Each GPIO output pin draws from this power source an additional 3 to 16 mA, depending on how it is used. For more information about this, see Chapter 10.

Powered USB Hubs

If your power budget is stretched by USB peripherals, you may want to consider the use of a *powered* USB hub. In this way, the *hub* rather than your Raspberry Pi provides the necessary power to the downstream peripherals. The hub is especially attractive for the Model A because it provides additional ports.

Again, take into account that not all USB hubs work with (Raspbian) Linux. The kernel needs to cooperate with connected USB hubs, so software support is critical. The following web page lists known working USB hubs:

```
http://elinux.org/RPi_Powered_USB_Hubs
```

Power Adapters

This section pertains mostly to the Model B because the Model A is easily supported by a USB 2 port. We'll first look at an unsuitable source of power and consider the factors for finding suitable units.

An Unsuitable Supply

The example shown in Figure 2-4 was purchased on eBay for $1.18 with free shipping (see the upcoming warning about fakes). For this reason, it was tempting to use it.

Figure 2-4. *Model A1265 Apple adapter*

This is an adapter/charger with the following ratings:

- *Model*: A1265

- *Input*: 100–240 VAC

- *Output*: 5 V, 1 A

When plugged in, the Raspberry Pi's power LED immediately lights up, which is a good sign for an adapter (vs. a charger). A fast rise time on the power leads to successful power-on resets. When the voltage was measured, the reading was +4.88 V on the +5 V supply. While not ideal, it is within the range of acceptable voltages. (The voltage must be between 4.75 and 5.25 V.)

9

The Apple unit seemed to work fairly well when HDMI graphics were *not* being utilized (using serial console, SSH, or VNC). However, I found that when HDMI was used and the GPU had work to do (move a window across the desktop, for example), the system would tend to seize up. This clearly indicates that the adapter does not fully deliver or regulate well enough.

■ **Caution**   Be very careful of counterfeit Apple chargers/adapters. The Raspberry Pi Foundation has seen returned units damaged by these. For a video and further information, see www.raspberrypi.org/archives/2151.

E-book Adapters

Some people have reported good success using e-book power adapters. I have also successfully used a 2 A Kobo charger.

Best Power Source

While it is possible to buy USB power adapters at low prices, it is wiser to spend more on a high-quality unit. It is not worth trashing your Raspberry Pi or experiencing random failures for the sake of saving a few dollars.

If you lack an oscilloscope, you won't be able to check how clean or dirty your supply current is. A better power adapter is cheaper than an oscilloscope. A shaky/noisy power supply can lead to all kinds of obscure and intermittent problems.

A good place to start is to simply Google "recommended power supply Raspberry Pi." Do your research and include your USB peripherals in the power budget. Remember that wireless USB adapters consume a lot of current—up to 500 mA.

■ **Note**   A random Internet survey reveals a range of 330 mA to 480 mA for wireless USB adapter current consumption.

Voltage Test

If you have a DMM or other suitable voltmeter, it is worthwhile to perform a test after powering up the Pi. This is probably the very first thing you should do, if you are experiencing problems.

Follow these steps to perform a voltage test:

1. Plug the Raspberry Pi's micro-USB port into the power adapter's USB port.

2. Plug in the power adapter.

3. Measure the voltage between P1-02 (+5 V) and P1-25 (Ground): expect +4.75 to +5.25 V.

4. Measure the voltage between P1-01 (+3.3 V) and P1-25 (Ground): expect +3.135 to +3.465 V.

■ **Caution** Be very careful with your multimeter probes around the pins of P1. *Be especially careful not to short the +5 V to the +3.3 V pin*, even for a fraction of a second. Doing so will zap your Pi! If you feel nervous or shaky about this, leave it alone. You may end up doing more harm than good. As a precaution, put a piece of wire insulation (or spaghetti) over the +3.3 V pin.

The left side of Figure 2-5 shows the DMM probes testing for +5 V on header strip P1. Again, be very careful not to touch more than one pin at a time when performing these measurements. *Be particularly careful not to short between 5 V and 3.3 V.* To avoid a short-circuit, use a piece of wire insulation, heat shrink tubing, or even a spaghetti noodle over the other pin.

Figure 2-5. *Measuring voltages*

The right side of Figure 2-5 shows the positive DMM probe moved to P1-01 to measure the +3.3 V pin. Appendix B lists the ATX power supply standard voltage levels, which include +5 ± 0.25 V and +3.3 ± 0.165 V.

Battery Power

Because of the small size of the Raspberry Pi, it may be desirable to run it from battery power. Doing so requires a regulator and some careful planning. To meet the Raspberry Pi requirements, you must form a power budget. Once you know your maximum current, you can flesh out the rest. The following example assumes that 1 A is required.

Requirements

For clarity, let's list our battery power requirements:

- Voltage   5 V, within ± 0.25 V
- Current   1 A

Headroom

The simplest approach is to use the linear LM7805 as the 5 V regulator. But there are some disadvantages:

- There must be some headroom above the input voltage (about 2 V).

- Allowing too much headroom increases the power dissipation in the regulator, resulting in wasted battery power.

- A lower maximum output current can also result.

Your batteries should provide a minimum input of 5+2 V (7 V). Any lower input voltage to the regulator will result in the regulator "dropping out" and dipping below 5 V. Clearly, a 6 V battery input will not do.

LM7805 Regulation

Figure 2-6 shows a very simple battery circuit using the LM7805 linear regulator. Resistor R_L represents the load (the Raspberry Pi).

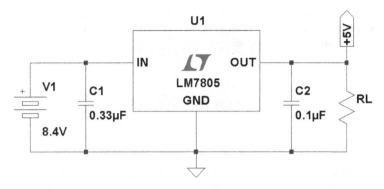

Figure 2-6. *Regulated battery supply*

The 8.4 V battery is formed from seven NiCad cells in series, each producing 1.2 V. The 8.4 V input allows the battery to drop to a low of 7 V before the minimum headroom of 2 V is violated.

Depending on the exact 7805 regulator part chosen, a typical heat-sinked parameter set might be as follows:

- *Input voltage*: 7–25 V

- *Output voltage*: 1.5 A (heat-sinked)

- *Operating temperature*: 125°C

Be sure to use a heat sink on the regulator so that it can dissipate heat energy to the surrounding air. Without one, the regulator can enter a thermal shutdown state, reducing current flow to prevent its own destruction. When this happens, the output voltage will drop below +5 V.

Keep in mind that the amount of power dissipated by the battery is more than that received by the load. If we assume that the Raspberry Pi is consuming 700 mA, a minimum of 700 mA is also drawn from the battery through the regulator (and it could be slightly higher). Realize that the regulator is dissipating additional energy because of its higher input voltage. The total power dissipated by the regulator and the load is as follows:

$$P_d = P_L + P_R$$
$$= 5\ V \times 0.7\ A + (8.4\ V - 5\ V) \times 0.7\ A$$
$$= 3.5\ W + 2.38\ W$$
$$= 5.88\ W$$

The regulator must dissipate the difference between the input and the output voltages (2.38 W). This additional energy heats up the regulator with the energy being given away at the heat sink. Because of this, designers avoid using a high input voltage on linear regulator circuits.

If the regulator is rated at a maximum of 1.5 A at 7 V (input), the power maximum for the regulator is about 10.5 W. If we apply an input voltage of 8.4 V instead of 7, we can derive what our 5 V maximum current will be:

$$I_{max} = \frac{P_{max}}{V_{in}}$$
$$= \frac{10.5\,W}{8.4\,V}$$
$$= 1.25\,A$$

From this, we find that the 8.4 V battery regulator circuit can provide a maximum of 1.25 A at the output, without exceeding the regulator's power rating. Multiply 8.4 V by 1.25 A to convince yourself that this equals 10.5 W.

DC-DC Buck Converter

If the application is designed for data acquisition, for example, it is desirable to have it run as long as possible on a given set of batteries or charge cycle. A switching regulator may be more suitable than the linear regulator.

Figure 2-7 shows a very small PCB that is about 1.5 SD cards in length. This unit was purchased from eBay for $1.40, with free shipping. At these prices, why would you build one?

Figure 2-7. DC-DC buck converter

They are also simple to use. You have + and – input connections and + and – output connections. Feed power in at one voltage and get power out at another voltage. This is so simple that you'll forgive me if I omit the diagram for it.

But don't immediately wire it up to your Raspberry Pi, until you have calibrated the output voltage. While it *might* come precalibrated for 5 V, it is best not to count on it. If the unit produces a higher voltage, you might fry the Pi.

The regulated output voltage is easily adjusted by a multiturn trim pot on the PCB. Adjust the pot while you read your DMM.

The specifications for the unit I purchased are provided in Table 2-1 for your general amusement. Notice the wide range of input voltages and the fact that it operates at a temperature as low as –40°C. The wide range of input voltages and current up to 3 A clearly makes this a great device to attach to solar panels that might vary widely in voltage.

Table 2-1. *DC-DC buck converter specifications*

Parameter	Min	Max	Units	Parameter	Min	Max	Units
Input voltage	4.00	35.0	Volts	Output ripple		30.9	mA
Input current		3.0	Amps	Load regulation	±0.5		%
Output voltage	1.23	30.0	Volts	Voltage regulation	±2.5		%
Conversion efficiency		92	%	Working temperature	–40	+85	°C
Switching frequency		150	kHz	PCB size		45×20×12	mm
				Net weight		10	g

The specification claims up to a 92% conversion efficiency. Using 15 V on the input, I performed my own little experiment with measurements. With the unit adjusted to produce 5.1 V at the output, the readings shown in Table 2-2 were taken.

Table 2-2. *Readings taken from experiment*

Parameter	Input	Output	Units
Voltage	15.13	5.10	Volts
Current	0.190	0.410	Amps
Power	2.87	2.09	Watts

From the table we expected to see more power used on the input side (2.87 W). The power used on the output side was 2.09 W. The efficiency then becomes a matter of division:

$$\frac{2.09}{2.87} = 0.728$$

From this we can conclude that the measured conversion efficiency was about 72.8%.

How well could we have done if we used the LM7805 regulator? The following is a best case estimate, since I don't have an actual current reading for that scenario. But we do know that at least as much current that flows out of the regulator must flow into it (likely more). So what is the absolute best that the LM7805 regulator could theoretically do? Let's apply the same current draw of 410 mA for the Raspberry Pi at 5.10 V, as shown in Table 2-3. (This was operating without HDMI output in use.)

Table 2-3. *Hypothetical LM7805 power use*

Parameter	Input	Output	Units
Voltage	7.1	5.10	Volts
Current	0.410	0.410	Amps
Power	2.91	2.09	Watts

The power efficiency for this best case scenario amounts to this:

$$\frac{2.09}{2.91} = 0.718$$

The absolute best case efficiency for the LM7805 regulator is 71.8%. But this is achieved at its *optimal* input voltage. Increasing the input voltage to 12 V causes the power dissipation to rise considerably, resulting in a 42.5% efficiency (this calculation is left to the reader as an exercise). Attempting to operate the LM7805 regulator at 15.13 V, as we did with the buck converter, would cause the efficiency to drop to less than 33.7%. Clearly, the buck converter is much more efficient at converting power from a higher voltage source.

Signs of Insufficient Power

In the forums, it has been reported that ping sometimes doesn't work from the desktop (with HDMI), yet works OK in console mode.[42] Additionally, I have seen that desktop windows can freeze if you move them (HDMI). As you start to move the terminal window, for example, the motion would freeze part way through, as if the mouse stopped working.

These are signs of the Raspberry Pi being power starved. The GPU consumes more power when it is active, performing accelerated graphics. Either the desktop freezes (GPU starvation) or the network interface fails (ping). There may be other symptoms related to HDMI activity.

Another problem that has been reported is resetting of the Raspberry Pi shortly after starting to boot. The board starts to consume more power as the kernel boots up, which can result in the Pi being starved.[43]

If you lose your Ethernet connection when you plug in a USB device, this too may be a sign of insufficient power.[44]

While it may seem that a 1 A power supply should be enough to supply a 700 mA Raspberry Pi, you will be better off using a 2 A supply instead. Many power supplies simply don't deliver their full advertised ratings.

The micro-USB cable is something else to suspect. Some are manufactured with thin conductors that can result in a significant voltage drop. Measuring the voltage as shown previously in the "Voltage Test" section may help diagnose that. Try a higher-quality cable to see whether there is an improvement.

No Power

If your Pi appears dead, even though power is present at the input, the input polyfuse could have blown. If this was a recent event, allow the unit to cool down. The polymer in the fuse recrystallizes, but this can take several hours. If you think the F3 poly fuse is permanently destroyed, see the Linux wiki page[45] for how to test it.

■ ■ ■

## CHAPTER 3

Header Strips, LEDs, and Reset

In this chapter, an inventory of the Raspberry Pi header strips, LEDs, and reset button connections is covered. These are important interfaces from the Pi to the outside world. You may want to use a bookmark for Table 3-3, which outlines the general purpose input/output (GPIO) pins on header strip P1.

Status LEDs

The Model A Raspberry Pi has a subset of the Model B LED indicators because it lacks the Ethernet port. The Model B has three additional LEDs, each showing the network status. Table 3-1 provides a list of LED statuses.

Table 3-1. *Status LEDs*

LED	Color	Model A	Model B	Comment
ACT	Green	OK	ACT	SD card access activity
PWR	Red	Yes	Yes	Power supply
FDX	Green	N/A	Yes	LAN: Full duplex
LNK	Green	N/A	Yes	LAN: Link
100	Yellow	N/A	100	Labeled incorrectly on Rev 1.0 as 10M: 10/100 Mbit link

OK or ACT LED

This green LED indicates SD card I/O activity. This active low LED is internally driven by the kernel on GPIO 16 (see the kernel source file bcm2708.c in arm/mach-bcm2708).

PWR LED

This red LED simply indicates that the Raspberry Pi has power. Figure 3-1 shows that the power LED is supplied from the 3.3 V regulator.[14] Consequently, the LED indicates only that power is arriving through the 3.3 V regulator.

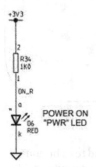

Figure 3-1. *Power LED*

     The power LED indicator is not necessarily an indication that the power is *good*. It simply indicates that power is present. The LED can be lit and still not have sufficient voltage present for the CPU to operate correctly.

     If there is any doubt about how good the power supply is, refer to the "Voltage Test" section in Chapter 2, which has information about how to perform a voltage test.

FDX LED

This green LED indicates that the Ethernet port is operating in *full-duplex* mode.

LNK LED

This green LED indicates that the Ethernet port has an active link-level status.

10M or 10/100 LED

Model B Rev 1.0 had this LED incorrectly labelled as *10M*. The correct label is 100, which is found on Rev 2.0 boards. This yellow LED indicates that the 100 Mbit link is active (otherwise, it is a 10 Mbit link).

Header P1

The Raspberry Pi includes a 13x2 pin strip identified as P1, which exposes GPIO pins. This includes the I2C, SPI, and UART peripherals as well as the +3.3 V, +5.0 V, and ground connections. Table 3-2 shows the pin assignments for the Model B, Rev 1.0 PCB.

Table 3-2. *Rev 1.0 GPIO Header Connector P1 (Top View)*

Lower Left			Upper Left
3.3 V power	P1-01	P1-02	5 V power
GPIO 0 (I2C0_SDA)+*R1=1.8k*	P1-03	P1-04	5 V power
GPIO 1 (I2C0_SCL)+*R2=1.8k*	P1-05	P1-06	Ground
GPIO 4 (GPCLK 0/1-Wire)	P1-07	P1-08	GPIO 14 (TXD)
Ground	P1-09	P1-10	GPIO 15 (RXD)
GPIO 17	P1-11	P1-12	GPIO 18 (PCM_CLK)
GPIO 21 (PCM_DOUT)	P1-13	P1-14	Ground
GPIO 22	P1-15	P1-16	GPIO 23
3.3 V power	P1-17	P1-18	GPIO 24
GPIO 10 (MOSI)	P1-19	P1-20	Ground
GPIO 9 (MISO)	P1-21	P1-22	GPIO 25
GPIO 11 (SCKL)	P1-23	P1-24	GPIO 8 (CE0)
Ground	P1-25	P1-26	GPIO 7 (CE1)
Lower Right			**Upper Right**

■ **Caution** The Model A can supply a maximum of 500 mA from the +5 V pins of P1. The model B has a lower maximum limit of 300 mA. These limits are due to the fusible link F3 on the PCB (shown previously in Figure 2-2 in Chapter 2). Note also for both models, the +3.3 V pins of P1 and P5 are limited to a maximum of 50 mA. This is the remaining capacity of the onboard voltage regulator. GPIO currents also draw from this resource. (See Figure 2-3.)

Table 3-3 shows the connections for the Model B revision 2.0. According to the Raspberry Pi website[14], these pin assignments are not expected to change beyond Rev 2.0 in future revisions. The additional Rev 2.0 header P5 is shown in Table 3-4.

■ **Note** Chapter 5 provides more information on identifying your Raspberry Pi. If you have an early pre Rev 2.0 board, be aware that the GPIO pins differ.

Table 3-3. *Rev 2.0 GPIO Header Connector P1 (Top View)*

Lower Left			Upper Left
3.3 V power, 50 mA max	P1-01	P1-02	5 V power
GPIO 2 (I2C1_SDA1)+R1=1.8k	P1-03	P1-04	*5 V power*
GPIO 3 (I2C1_SCL1)+R2=1.8k	P1-05	P1-06	Ground
GPIO 4 (GPCLK 0/1-Wire)	P1-07	P1-08	GPIO 14 (TXD0)
Ground	P1-09	P1-10	GPIO 15 (RXD0)
GPIO 17 (GEN0)	P1-11	P1-12	GPIO 18 (PCM_CLK/GEN1)
GPIO 27 (GEN2)	P1-13	P1-14	*Ground*
GPIO 22 (GEN3)	P1-15	P1-16	GPIO 23 (GEN4)
3.3 V power, 50 mA max	P1-17	P1-18	GPIO 24 (GEN5)
GPIO 10 (SPI_MOSI)	P1-19	P1-20	*Ground*
GPIO 9 (SPI_MISO)	P1-21	P1-22	GPIO 25 (GEN6))
GPIO 11 (SPI_SCKL)	P1-23	P1-24	GPIO 8 (CE0_N)
Ground	P1-25	P1-26	GPIO 7 (CE1_N)
Lower Right			**Upper Right**

Table 3-4. *Rev 2.0 P5 Header (Top View)*

Lower Left			Upper Left
(Square) 5 V	P5-01	P5-02	3.3 V, 50 mA
GPIO 28	P5-03	P5-04	GPIO 29
GPIO 30	P5-05	P5-06	GPIO 31
Ground	P5-07	P5-08	Ground
Lower Right			**Upper Right**

Safe Mode

If your Raspbian SD image supports it, a *safe mode* can be activated when needed. The New Out of Box Software (NOOBS) image still appears to support this feature.

Pin P1-05, GPIO 3 is special to the boot sequence for Rev 2.0 models. (This is GPIO 1 on the pre Rev 2.0 Model B.) Grounding this pin or jumpering this to P1-06 (ground) causes the boot sequence to use a safe mode boot procedure. If the pin is used for some other purpose, you can prevent this with configuration parameter avoid_safe_mode=1. Be very careful that you don't accidentally ground a power pin (like P1-01 or P1-02) when you do use it.

If yours fails to respond to safe mode, it may be due to a manufacturing error. See this message:

```
www.raspberrypi.org/phpBB3/viewtopic.php?f=29&t=12007
```

In that thread, it is suggested that you check the following:

```
$ vcgencmd otp_dump | grep 30:
30:00000002
```

If you see the value 2, it means that the firmware thinks this is a Rev 1.0 board (even though it may be a Rev 2.0). When that applies, it will not support the safe mode sequence. Newer Rev 2.0 Pis do not have this issue.

When safe mode is invoked by the jumper, the config.txt file is ignored except for the avoid_safe_mode parameter. Additionally, this mode overrides the kernel command line, and kernel_emergency.img is loaded. If this file is unavailable, kernel.img is used instead.

The intent of this feature is to permit the user to overcome configuration problems without having to edit the SD card on another machine in order to make a correction. The booted emergency kernel is a BusyBox image with /boot mounted so that adjustments can be made. Additionally, the /dev/mmcblk0p2 root file system partition can be fixed up or mounted if necessary.

Logic Levels

The logic level used for GPIO pins is 3.3 V and is *not* tolerant of 5 V TTL logic. The Raspberry Pi PCB is designed to be plugged into PCB extension cards or otherwise carefully interfaced to 3 V logic. Input voltage parameters V_{IL} and V_{IH} are described in Chapter 10. This feature of the Pi makes it an interesting case study as we interface it to the outside world.

GPIO Configuration at Reset

The Raspberry Pi GPIO pins can be configured by software control to be input or output, to have pull-up or pull-down resistors, or to assume some specialized peripheral function. After reset, only GPIO 14 and 15 are assigned a special function (UART). After boot up, however, software can even reconfigure the UART pins as required.

When a GPIO pin is configured for output, there is a limited amount of current that it can drive (source or sink). By default, each P1 GPIO is configured to use an 8 mA driver, when the pin is configured as an output. Chapter 10 has more information on the software control of this.

■ **Note**   Raspbian 1-Wire bus is GPIO 4 (GPCLK0) Pin P1-07.

1-Wire Driver

The default GPIO pin used for the 1-Wire driver is GPIO 4. This is hard-coded in the following kernel source file:

```
arch/arm/mach-bcm2708/bcm2708.c
```

If you need to change this default, alter the line in bcm2708.c that defines the macro W1_GPIO:

```
#define  W1_GPIO  4
```

Then rebuild your kernel.

Header P5

Be careful with the orientation of this Model B Rev 2.0 header strip. See Figure 3-2: while looking down at P1, with its pin 1 at the lower left, the P5 strip has its pin 1 at the upper left (note the square pad on either side of the PCB).

Figure 3-2. P5's pin 1 location on the Rev 2.0 Model B

As a practical matter, I found that the pins for P5 can be soldered into the PCB with some care (they are not included). However, the proximity of P5 to P1 makes it impossible to plug in a header connector to P1 and P5 at the same time. With the pins installed, it is possible to use individual wire plugs on the pins as needed. I ended up plugging in a dual-wire plug on P5-04 and P5-06, which is one row away from P1. These wires were then brought out to connectors on a wood strip for easier access.

By default, GPIO pins 28 through 31 are configured for driving 16 mA. (Chapter 10 has more information about this.)

Reset

In the revision 2.0 Raspberry Pi, a reset circuit was implemented, as shown in Figure 3-4.[11] To complete the reset circuit, attach a push button to pins 1 and 2 of P6, as shown in Figure 3-3.[14]

Figure 3-3. *Model B Rev 2.0 P6*

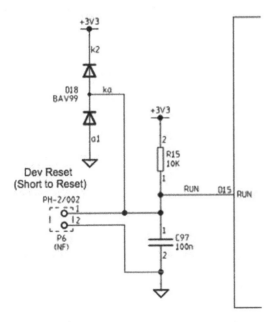

Figure 3-4. *Reset circuit*

To actuate the reset, P6 pin 1 is short-circuited to P6 pin 2. This resets the BCM2835 SoC chip. This is something you will want to avoid using while Raspbian Linux is up and running. Use reset as a last resort to avoid losing file content.

## CHAPTER 4

SDRAM

The Model B Rev 2.0 Raspberry Pi has 512 MB of SDRAM, while the older revisions and remaining models have 256 MB. Contrast this to the AVR class ATmega168p, which has 1 KB of static RAM. *SDRAM* is *synchronous dynamic random access memory*, which synchronizes with the system bus for improved performance. It uses a form of pipelining to gain this advantage.

There isn't much about the memory hardware that concerns the average Pi developer. However, in this chapter, you'll examine some useful Raspbian Linux kernel interfaces that inform us how that memory is utilized. You'll also examine how to access the memory-mapped ARM peripherals directly from your Linux application.

/proc/meminfo

The pseudo file /proc/meminfo provides us with information about memory utilization. This information varies somewhat by architecture and the compile options used for that kernel. Let's study an example that is produced by Raspbian Linux, on the Raspberry Pi:

```
$ cat /proc/meminfo
MemTotal:        448996 kB
MemFree:         340228 kB
Buffers:          14408 kB
Cached:           58532 kB
SwapCached:           0 kB
Active:           45948 kB
Inactive:         51564 kB
Active(anon):     24680 kB
Inactive(anon):     820 kB
Active(file):     21268 kB
Inactive(file):   50744 kB
Unevictable:          0 kB
Mlocked:              0 kB
SwapTotal:       102396 kB
SwapFree:        102396 kB
Dirty:                0 kB
Writeback:            0 kB
AnonPages:        24584 kB
```

```
Mapped:          20056 kB
Shmem:             932 kB
Slab:             6088 kB
SReclaimable:     2392 kB
SUnreclaim:       3696 kB
KernelStack:      1216 kB
PageTables:       1344 kB
NFS_Unstable:        0 kB
Bounce:              0 kB
WritebackTmp:        0 kB
CommitLimit:    326892 kB
Committed_AS:   215104 kB
VmallocTotal:   188416 kB
VmallocUsed:       744 kB
VmallocChunk:   186852 kB
```

All of the memory values shown have the units *KB* to the right of them, indicating kilo (1,024) bytes.

This next example was taken from a Model A Raspberry Pi, with 256 MB:[63]

```
$cat/proc/meminfo
MemTotal:       190836 kB
MemFree:        151352 kB
Buffers:          7008 kB
Cached:          20640 kB
SwapCached:          0 kB
Active:          14336 kB
Inactive:        18648 kB
Active(anon):     5468 kB
Inactive(anon):      0 kB
Active(file):     8868 kB
Inactive(file):  18648 kB
Unevictable:         0 kB
Mlocked:             0 kB
SwapTotal:           0 kB
SwapFree:            0 kB
Dirty:               0 kB
Writeback:           0 kB
AnonPages:        5348 kB
Mapped:           6512 kB
Shmem:             136 kB
Slab:             3712 kB
SReclaimable:     1584 kB
SUnreclaim:       2128 kB
KernelStack:       944 kB
PageTables:        620 kB
NFS_Unstable:        0 kB
```

```
Bounce:              0 kB
WritebackTmp:        0 kB
CommitLimit:     95416 kB
Committed_AS:    57876 kB
VmallocTotal:   188416 kB
VmallocUsed:       704 kB
VmallocChunk:   186852 kB
```

Many of these values are noticeably smaller.

In the sections that follow, a Model B to Model A comparison is provided. In some cases, the comparison isn't meaningful because the values represent activity that has or has not occurred. For example, the value for AnonPages is going to depend on the mix of commands and applications that have run. But values from both models are provided for completeness. Other values such as MemTotal can be meaningfully compared, however.

MemTotal

The MemTotal line indicates the total amount of memory available, minus a few reserved binary regions. Note that memory allocated to the GPU is not factored into MemTotal. Some may choose to allocate the minimum of 16 MB to the GPU to make more memory available.

	Model B	Model A
MemTotal	448,996 KB	190,836 KB

If we break this down a bit further, accounting for memory allocated to the GPU (see Chapter 2 of *Raspberry Pi System Software Reference* [Apress, 2014] for more details), we find that there is about 9.5 MB (1.9%) of memory that is unaccounted for, as shown in Table 4-1.

Table 4-1. GPU and Main Memory Breakdown

Memory	Model B	Comments
MemTotal	448,996 KB	/proc/meminfo
gpu_mem	65,536 KB	/boot/config.txt
Total	514,532 KB	502.5 MB
Unaccounted for	9,756 KB	9.5 MB

MemFree

MemFree normally represents the sum of LowFree + HighFree memory in kilobytes on the Intel x86 platform. For ARM, this simply represents the amount of memory available to user space programs.

	Model B	Model A
MemFree	340,228 KB	151,352 KB

The Model B has 332.25 MB for application programs, which amounts to about 64.9% (Rev 2.0). The Model A values indicate about 57.7% of the memory is available.

Buffers

This value represents temporary buffers used within the kernel for raw disk blocks, and so forth. This value should not get much larger than about 20 MB or so.[27]

	Model B	Model A
Buffers	14,408 KB	7,008 KB

Cached

This value represents the read file content that has been cached (page cache). This does not include the content reported for SwapCached.

	Model B	Model A
Cached	58,532 KB	20,640 KB

SwapCached

The value shown for SwapCached represents memory that was swapped out and is now swapped back in. For efficiency, these memory pages are still represented by swap disk space, should they be needed again.

	Model B	Model A
SwapCached	0 KB	0 KB

The fact that the value is reported as zero is a happy sign that no swapping has occurred, or is no longer pertinent.

Active

The Active memory value represents recently used memory that is not reclaimed, unless absolutely necessary.

	Model B	Model A
Active	45,948 KB	14,336 KB

Inactive

This value represents memory that is not active and is likely to be reclaimed when memory is needed.

	Model B	Model A
Inactive	51,564 KB	18,648 KB

Active(anon)

This value represents memory that is not backed up by a file and is active. Active memory is not reclaimed unless absolutely necessary.

	Model B	Model A
Active(anon)	24,680 KB	5,468 KB

Inactive(anon)

This value represents memory that is not backed up by a file and is not active. Inactive memory is eligible to be reclaimed if memory is required.

	Model B	Model A
Inactive(anon)	820 KB	0 KB

Active(file)

This value represents file-backed memory, which is active. Active memory is reclaimed only if absolutely required.

	Model B	Model A
Active(file)	21,268 KB	8,868 KB

Inactive(file)

This value represents inactive memory that is backed by a file. Inactive memory is eligible for reclamation, when memory is required.

	Model B	Model A
Inactive(file)	50,744 KB	18,648 KB

Unevictable

This amount reflects the total amount of memory that cannot be reclaimed. Memory that is locked, for example, cannot be reclaimed.

	Model B	Model A
Unevictable	0 KB	0 KB

Mlocked

This value reports the amount of locked memory.

	Model B	Model A
Mlocked	0 KB	0 KB

SwapTotal

This value reports the total amount of swap space available in kilobytes.

	Model B	Model A
SwapTotal	102,396 KB	0 KB

SwapFree

This value reports the remaining amount of swap space available in kilobytes.

	Model B	Model A
SwapFree	102,396 KB	0 KB

Dirty

This value represents the kilobytes of memory that have been modified and are waiting to be written to disk.

	Model B	Model A
Dirty	0 KB	0 KB

Writeback

This value reports the amount of memory in kilobytes being written back to disk.

	Model B	Model A
Writeback	0 KB	0 KB

AnonPages

This represents the non-file-backed pages of memory mapped into user space.

	Model B	Model A
AnonPages	24,584 KB	5,348 KB

Mapped

This value reports the files that have been mapped into memory. This may include library code.

	Model B	Model A
Mapped	20,056 KB	6,512 KB

Shmem

This parameter does not appear to be documented well. However, it represents the amount of shared memory in kilobytes

	Model B	Model A
Shmem	932 KB	136 KB

Slab

This parameter is described as "in-kernel data structures cache."[27]

	Model B	Model A
Slab	6,088 KB	3,712 KB

SReclaimable

This parameter is described as "Part of Slab that might be reclaimed, such as caches."[27]

	Model B	Model A
SReclaimable	2,392 KB	1,584 KB

SUnreclaim

This parameter is described as "Part of Slab that cannot be reclaimed [under] memory pressure."[27]

	Model B	Model A
SUnreclaim	3,696 KB	2,128 KB

KernelStack

This value reports the memory used by the kernel stack(s).

	Model B	Model A
KernelStack	1,216 KB	944 KB

PageTables

This value reports the amount of memory required by the page tables used in the kernel. Clearly, with more memory to manage, there is more memory dedicated to page tables.

	Model B	Model A
PageTables	1,344 KB	620 KB

NFS_Unstable

This value represents "NFS pages sent to the server, but not yet committed to stable storage."[27] This example data suggests that NFS is not being used.

	Model B	Model A
NFS_Unstable	0 KB	0 KB

Bounce

This reports the memory used for "block device bounce buffers."[27]

	Model B	Model A
Bounce	0 KB	0 KB

WritebackTmp

This parameter reports the memory used by FUSE for "temporary writeback buffers."[27]

	Model B	Model A
WritebackTmp	0 KB	0 KB

CommitLimit

The documentation states:

> *Based on the overcommit ratio (vm.overcommit_ratio), this is the total*
> *amount of memory currently available to be allocated on the system.*
> *This limit is only adhered to if strict overcommit accounting is enabled*
> *(mode 2 in vm.overcommit_memory). The CommitLimit is calculated with*
> *the following formula:*[27]

CommitLimit = (vm.overcommit_ratio × Physical RAM) + Swap

For example, a system with 1 GB of physical RAM and 7 GB of swap with a
vm.overcommit_ratio of 30 would yield a CommitLimit of 7.3 GB. For more details,
see the memory overcommit documentation in vm/overcommitaccounting.

The formula can be written as follows:

$$C = (R \times r) + S.$$

The elements of this formula are described here:

- C is the overcommit limit.
- R is the physical RAM available (MemTotal).
- S is the swap space available (SwapTotal).
- r is the overcommit ratio percent (expressed as a fraction).

The overcommit ratio, r, is not reported in the /proc/meminfo data. To obtain that
ratio, we consult another pseudo file. This example was taken from a Rev 2.0 Model B, but
it appears to be a value common to all Pis:

```
$ cat /proc/sys/vm/overcommit_ratio
50
```

The value 50 is to be interpreted as r = 0.50 (50%).

Using the overcommit formula, the value for S can be computed for the swap space
available:

$$
\begin{aligned}
S &= C - (R \times r) \\
&= 326892 - (448996 \times 0.50) \\
&= 326892 - 262144 \\
&= 102394 \ KB
\end{aligned}
$$

This fits within 2 KB of the SwapTotal value of 102,396 KB reported by /proc/meminfo.

The overcommit ratio is configurable by the user, by writing a value into the pseudo file. This example changes the ratio to 35%:

```
$ sudo -i
# echo 35 >/proc/sys/vm/overcommit_ratio
# cat /proc/sys/vm/overcommit_ratio
35
```

The CommitLimit values reported by our example Raspberry Pi sessions are shown in Table 4-2 for comparison purposes. A Model B pre Rev 2.0 version is also included here for comparison.

Table 4-2. *Example Model B to Model A Memory Comparisons*

	Model B Rev 2.0	Model B Pre 2.0	Model A
CommitLimit	326,892 KB	127,868 KB	95,416 KB
MemTotal	448,996 KB	124,672 KB	190,836 KB
SwapTotal	102,396 KB	65,532 KB	0 KB
Commit Ratio	50	50	50

With thanks to Dan Braun for providing the Model B Pre 2.0 data.

The value of the Model A commit ratio was calculated here since it wasn't available from the website. But if you calculate the swap space S for it, you arrive at the value of –2 KB, if you assume 50% for the commit ratio. This agrees with the 2 KB difference you saw earlier.

Committed_AS

This parameter is described as follows:

> *The amount of memory presently allocated on the system. The committed memory is a sum of all of the memory which has been allocated by processes, even if it has not been "used" by them as of yet. A process which malloc()'s 1 GB of memory, but only touches 300 MB of it will only show up as using 300 MB of memory even if it has the address space allocated for the entire 1 GB. This 1 GB is memory which has been "committed" to by the VM and can be used at any time by the allocating application. With strict overcommit enabled on the system (mode 2 in vm.overcommit_memory), allocations which would exceed the CommitLimit (detailed above) will not be permitted. This is useful if one needs to guarantee that processes will not fail due to lack of memory once that memory has been successfully allocated.*[27]

	Model B	Model A
Committed_AS	215,104 KB	57,876 KB

VmallocTotal

This represents the total amount of allocated virtual memory address space.

	Model B	Model A
VmallocTotal	188,416 KB	188,416 KB

VmallocUsed

This is the amount of virtual memory that is in use, reported in kilobytes.

	Model B	Model A
VmallocUsed	744 KB	704 KB

VmallocChunk

This value reports the largest size of a vmalloc area, in kilobytes.

	Model B	Model A
VmallocChunk	186,852 KB	186,852 KB

Physical Memory

Let's now turn our attention to the Raspberry Pi's physical memory layout. Normally, physical memory isn't a concern to application programmers, because the operating system and its drivers provide an abstract and often portable way to access them. However, when this support is absent, direct access to a peripheral like the PWM controller is necessary.

Figure 4-1 illustrates the physical addressing used on the Raspberry Pi. The SDRAM starts at physical address zero and works up to the ARM/GPU split point (Chapter 2 of *Raspberry Pi System Software Reference* [Apress, 2014] defines the split point). The ARM peripherals are mapped to physical memory starting at the address of 0x20000000. This starting address is of keen interest to Pi programmers.

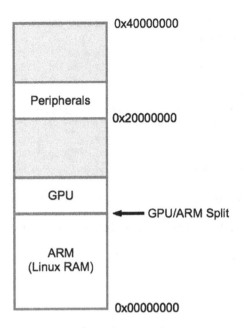

Figure 4-1. Physical memory layout

In the region labeled Peripherals, the offsets and addresses indicated in Table 4-3 are of interest to us.

Table 4-3. Peripheral Offsets for the Raspberry Pi

Peripheral	Offset	Address	Description	C Offset Macro
Base	0x00000000	0x20000000	Starting address	BCM2708_PERI_BASE
PADS_GPIO	0x00100000	0x20100000	PADS base	PADS_GPIO_BASE
GPIO 00..27	0x0010002C	0x2010002C	GPIO 00..27 pads	PADS_GPIO_00_27
GPIO 28..45	0x00100030	0x20100030	GPIO 28..45 pads	PADS_GPIO_28_45
GPIO 46..53	0x00100034	0x20100034	GPIO 46..53 pads	PADS_GPIO_46_53
Clock	0x00101000	0x20101000	Clock registers	CLK_BASE
GPIO	0x00200000	0x20200000	GPIO registers	GPIO_BASE
GPPUD	0x00200025	0x20200025	Pull-up enable	
GPPUDCLK0	0x00200026	0x20200026	Pull-up clock 0	
GPPUDCLK1	0x00200027	0x20200027	Pull-up clock 1	
PWM	0x0020C000	0x2020C000	PWM registers	PWM_BASE

39

Throughout this book, you'll see the macros BCM2708_PERI_BASE and GPIO_BASE, for example, used in programs that access the peripherals directly.

Memory Mapping

To gain access to physical memory under Linux, we make use of the /dev/mem character device and the mmap(2) system call. The /dev/mem node is shown here:

```
$ ls -l /dev/mem
crw-r----T 1 root kmem 1, 1 Dec 31 1969 /dev/mem
```

From the ownership information shown, it is immediately obvious that you'll need root privileges to access it. This is sensible given that a process can cause havoc with direct access to the physical memory. Clearly, the Pi developer should exercise caution in what the applications do with it.

The mmap(2) system call API is shown here:

```
#include <sys/mman.h>

void *mmap(
    void        *addr,      /* Address to use */
    size_t      length,     /* Number of bytes to access */
    int         prot,       /* Memory protection */
    int         flags,      /* Option flags */
    int         fd,         /* Opened file descriptor */
    off_t       offset      /* Starting off set */
) ;
```

Rather than look at all the options and flags available to this somewhat complicated system call, let's look at the ones that we use in the following code:

```
static char *map = 0;

static void
gpio_init() {
    int fd;
    char *map;

    fd = open("/dev/mem",O_RDWR|O_SYNC) ;    /* Needs root access */
    if ( fd < 0 ) {
        perror("Opening /dev/mem") ;
        exit(1) ;
    }
```

```
map = (char *) mmap(
    NULL,                       /* Any address */
    BLOCK_SIZE,                 /* # of bytes */
    PROT_READ|PROT_WRITE,
    MAP_SHARED,                 /* Shared */
    fd,                         /* /dev/mem */
    GPIO_BASE                   /* Offset to GPIO */
) ;

if ( (long)map == -1L ) {
    perror("mmap(/dev/mem)");
    exit(1) ;
}

close(fd);
ugpio = (volatile unsigned *)map;
}
```

The first thing performed in this code is to open the device driver node /dev/mem. It is opened for reading and writing (O_RDWR), and the option flag O_SYNC requests that any write(2) call to this file descriptor result in blocking the execution of the caller until it has completed.

Address

Next, the mmap(2) call is invoked. The address argument is provided with NULL (zero) so that the kernel can choose where to map it into the caller's address space. If the application were to specify a starting address to use and the kernel was not able use it, the system call would fail. The starting address is returned and assigned to the character pointer map in the preceding listing.

Length

Argument 2 is supplied with the macro BLOCK_SIZE in this example. This is the number of bytes you would like to map into your address space. This was defined earlier in the program as 4 KB:

```
#define BLOCK_SIZE (4*1024)
```

While the application may not need the full 4 KB of physical memory mapped, mmap(2) may insist on using a multiple of the page size. This can be verified on the command line as follows:

```
$ getconf PAGE_SIZE
4096
```

A program could determine this as well, by using the sysconf(2) system call:

```
#include <unistd.h>

...
long sz = sysconf(_SC_PAGESIZE);
```

Protection

The third mmap(2) argument is supplied with the flags PROT_READ and PROT_WRITE. This indicates that the application wants both read and write access to the memory-mapped region.

Flags

The flags argument is supplied with the value MAP_SHARED. This permits nonexclusive access to the underlying mapping.

File Descriptor

This argument supplies the underlying opened file to be mapped into memory. In this case, we map a region of physical ARM memory into our application by using the opened device driver node /dev/mem.

Offset

This last argument specifies the location in physical memory where we want to start our access. For the GPIO registers, it is the address 0x20200000.

Return Value

The return value, when successful, will be an application address that points to the physical memory region we asked for. The application programmer need not be concerned with what this address is, except to save and use it for access.

The return value is also used for indicating failure, so this should be checked and handled:

```
if ( (long) map == -1L ) {
    perror("mmap(/dev/mem)");
    exit(1);
}
```

The returned address (pointer) map is cast to a long integer and compared to -1L. This is the magic value that indicates that an error occurred. The error code is found in errno.

Volatile

The last section of this initialization code for GPIO assigns the address map to another variable, ugpio, as follows:

```
ugpio = (volatile unsigned *)map;
```

The value ugpio was defined earlier in the program:

```
static volatile unsigned *ugpio = 0;
```

There are two things noteworthy about this:

- The data type is an unsigned int (32 bits on the Pi).

- The pointed-to data is marked as *volatile*.

Since the Pis registers are 32 bits in size, it is often more convenient to access them as 32-bit words. The unsigned data type is perfect for this. But be careful with *offsets* in conjunction with this pointer, since they will be *word* offsets rather than byte offsets.

The volatile keyword tells the compiler not to optimize access to memory through the pointer variable. Imagine code that reads a peripheral register and reads the same register again later, to see whether an event has occurred. An optimizing compiler might say to itself, "I already have this value in CPU register R, so I'll just use that since it is faster." But the effect of this code is that it will never see a bit change in the peripheral's register because that data was not fetched back into a CPU register. The volatile keyword forces the compiler to retrieve the value even though it would be faster to use the value still found in a register.

Virtual Memory

In the previous section, you looked at how to access physical memory in an application, provided that you had the rights to do so (root or setuid). The Broadcom Corporation PDF manual "BCM2835 ARM Peripherals," page 5, also shows a *virtual* memory layout on the right. This should not be confused with the *physical* memory layout that you examined earlier. Virtual memory can be accessed through /dev/kmem driver node using mmap(2), but we won't be needing that in this book.

Final Thoughts on SDRAM

Some parameters such as Buffers impact the performance of Raspbian Linux on the Pi. From our comparison, we saw that the Model A seems to use about half of the buffering available to the Model B Rev 2.0 Pi. This is reasonable when limited memory has to be divided between operating system and application use.

Another performance area related to memory is how much SDRAM is dedicated to GPU use. This parameter is examined in Chapter 2 of *Raspberry Pi System Software Reference* (Apress, 2014).

Probably the most important aspect of memory allocation is how much memory is available to the developer's application programs. The value of `MemFree` is perhaps the most useful metric for this. When exceeding physical memory limits, the swapping parameters then become measurements of interest.

Finally, we took a detailed look at how to access the Raspberry Pi peripherals directly using `mmap(2)`. Until Raspbian Linux gains device drivers for peripherals such as PWM, the direct access technique will be necessary. Even with driver support, there are sometimes valid reasons to access the peripheral registers directly.

CHAPTER 5

CPU

The Raspberry Pi includes an ARM 700 MHz CPU. In this chapter, you'll first look at the versions of the Pi that have been released into the wild. Then after looking briefly at overclocking, you'll examine how the CPU is exploited by the Linux application.

Identification

Several revisions of the Pi have been released and sold. Table 5-1 lists the known revisions and some of the changes related to them.

Table 5-1. Board Identification[40, 41]

Code	Model	Rev.	RAM	P1-03	P1-05	P1-13	P5	Manuf.	Comments
0002	B	1.0	256 MB	GPIO0	GPIO1	GPIO21	N	Egoman?	
0003	B	1.0+	256 MB	GPIO0	GPIO1	GPIO21	N	Egoman?	Fuse mod and D14 removed
0004	B	2.0	256 MB	GPIO1	GPIO2	GPIO27	Y	Sony	
0005	B	2.0	256 MB	GPIO1	GPIO2	GPIO27	Y	Qisda	
0006	B	2.0	256 MB	GPIO1	GPIO2	GPIO27	Y	Egoman	
0007	A	2.0	256 MB	GPIO1	GPIO2	GPIO27	Y	Egoman	
0008	A	2.0	256 MB	GPIO1	GPIO2	GPIO27	Y	Sony	
0009	A	2.0	256 MB	GPIO1	GPIO2	GPIO27	Y	Qisda	
000d	B	2.0	512 MB	GPIO1	GPIO2	GPIO27	Y	Egoman	
000e	B	2.0	512 MB	GPIO1	GPIO2	GPIO27	Y	Sony	
000f	B	2.0	512 MB	GPIO1	GPIO2	GPIO27	Y	Qisda	

Once your Raspberry Pi has booted up in Raspbian Linux, you can check the board's identification with the following command:

```
$ cat /proc/cpuinfo
Processor       : ARMv6-compatible processor rev 7 (v6l)
BogoMIPS        : 697.95
Features        : swp half thumb fastmult vfp edsp java tls
CPU implementer : 0x41
CPU architecture: 7
CPU variant     : 0x0
CPU part        : 0xb76
CPU revision    : 7
Hardware        : BCM2708
Revision        : 000f
Serial          : 00000000f52b69d9
```

The preceding example reports a revision of 000f, which is a Rev 2.0 Pi.

Overclocking

Raspbian Linux for the Raspberry Pi is conservatively configured for reliability by default. Those with the need for speed can reconfigure it for increased performance but at the risk of less-reliable operation.

Raspbian Linux 3.6.11 provides a raspi-config menu of five CPU profiles. The profile None is the default:

Profile	ARM CPU	Core	SDRAM	Overvolt
None	700 MHz	250 MHz	400 MHz	0
Modest	800 MHz	250 MHz	400 MHz	0
Medium	900 MHz	250 MHz	450 MHz	2
High	950 MHz	250 MHz	450 MHz	6
Turbo	1 GHz	500 MHz	600 MHz	6

The raspi-config requires root privileges and is started as follows:

```
$ sudo raspi-config
```

The initial menu screen provides an overclock selection with the description Configure overclocking. Choosing that menu item opens another menu, allowing you to choose a profile.

Choosing a profile from this menu changes the following parameters in /boot/config.txt:

Parameter	None	Modest	Medium	High	Turbo
arm_freq=	700	800	900	950	1000
core_freq=	250	250	250	250	500
sdram_freq=	400	400	450	450	600
over_voltage=	0	0	2	6	6

When trading reliability for performance, these factors should be considered as it relates to your application:

- How critical is the application for
  - Correctness/accuracy
  - Uptime
- How does increased performance relate to the results?
  - Improved accuracy (Fourier transforms, real-time processing)
  - Increased number of measurements/sampling points
- What is the impact of failure?
- Will the unit perform reliably in all required temperatures (in an enclosure, outdoors)?

How do these performance profiles affect day-to-day performance? Developers are often concerned about compile times, so I did a simple compile-time test.

The test procedure used is as follows:

1. With raspi-config, configure the desired overclocking profile.
2. Reboot.
3. Change to the book's source code top-level directory.
4. Use the command make clobber.
5. Use the command time make.

Table 5-2 summarizes the results in seconds for compiling all projects for this book, using the different overclocking profiles. The elapsed times did not always improve (Real), but they can vary widely because of how I/O to the SD card occurs. The CPU time otherwise improved, with one small exception between Medium and High "User" CPU time.

Table 5-2. *Profile Compile Tests*

Profile	Real	User	System
None	56.641	23.730	3.520
Modest	37.475	22.330	3.510
Medium	40.127	20.830	3.360
High	49.318	20.980	3.240
Turbo	32.756	15.380	2.650

Everyone has a different appetite for speed. I usually favor reliability over speed, since failure and intermittent problems can cause "wild goose chases" and otherwise waste valuable time. Yet in some situations performance can be important enough to accept the risks. An application performing real-time Fourier transforms on audio might justify Turbo mode, for example.

Execution

Connected with the idea of the CPU is program execution itself. Before you look at program execution, you need to take high-level view of the execution context. Figure 5-1 shows the operating environment that an executing program operates within.

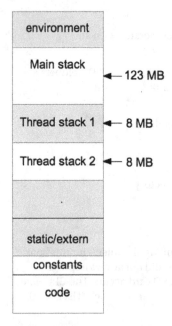

Figure 5-1. *Program execution context*

At the lowest end of the address space is the "text" region containing the program code. This region of virtual memory is read-only, containing read-only program constants in addition to executable code.

The next region (in increasing address) contains blocks of uninitialized arrays, buffers, static C variables, and extern storage.

At the high end of memory are environment variables for the program, like PATH. You can easily check this yourself by using getenv("PATH") and printing the returned address for it. Its address will likely be the highest address in your Raspberry Pi application, except possibly for another environment variable.

Below that, your main program's stack begins and grows downward. Each function call causes a new stack frame to be created below the current one.

If you now add a thread to the program, a new stack has to be allocated for it. Experiments on the Pi show that the first thread stack gets created approximately 123 MB below the main stack's beginning. A second thread has its stack allocated about 8 MB below the first. Each new thread's stack (by default) is allocated 8 MB of stack space.

Dynamically allocated memory gets allocated from the *heap*, which sits between the static/extern region and the bottom end of the stack.

Threads

Before threads were perfected under Linux, many application developers tended to avoid them. Now, however, there is little reason to.

Every attempt was made to keep the project programs in this book simple. This usually meant also avoiding threads. Yet, a few projects would have been more complicated without them. In the example using ØMQ, threads would have been present behind the scenes, even if we didn't see them in our application code.

With that introduction, let's take a crash course on the pthread API as it applies to Raspbian Linux.

pthread Headers

All pthread functions require the following header file:

```
#include <pthread.h>
```

When linking programs compiled to use pthreads, add the linker option:

-lpthread: Link with the pthread library.

pthread Error Handling

The pthread routines return zero when they succeed and *return an error code when they fail*. The value errno is *not* used for these calls.

The reason behind this is likely that it was thought that the traditional Unix errno approach would be phased out in the near future (at the time POSIX threads were being standardized). The original use of errno was as follows:

```
extern int errno;
```

However, this approach didn't work for threaded programs. Imagine two threads concurrently opening files with open(2), which sets the errno value upon failure. Both threads cannot share the same int value for errno.

Rather than change a vast body of code already using errno in this manner, other approaches were implemented to provide each thread with its own private copy of errno. This is one reason that programs today using errno must include the header file errno.h. The header file takes care of defining the thread specific reference to errno.

Because the pthread standard was developing before the errno solution generally emerged, the pthread library returns the error code directly when there is an error and returns zero when the call is a success. If Unix were to be rewritten from scratch today, all system calls would probably work this way.

pthread_create(3)

The function pthread_create(3) is used to create a new thread of execution. The function call looks more daunting than it really is:

```
int pthread_create(
  pthread_t *thread,
  const pthread_attr_t *attr,
  void *(*start_routine)(void *),
  void *arg
);
```

The call to pthread_create(3) creates a new stack, sets up registers, and performs other housekeeping. Let's describe the arguments:

> thread: This first argument is simply a pointer to a pthread_t variable to receive the created thread's ID value. The ID value allows you to query and control the created thread. If the call succeeds, the thread ID is returned to the calling program.

> attr: This is a pointer to a pthread_attr_t attribute object that supplies various options and parameters. If you can accept the defaults, simply supply zero or NULL.

> start_routine: As shown in the following code, this is simply the name of a start routine that accepts a void pointer and returns a void pointer.

arg: This generic pointer is passed to start_routine. It may point to anything of interest to the thread function (start_routine). Often this is a structure containing values, or in a C++ program, it can be the pointer to an object. If you don't need an argument value, supply zero (or NULL).

returns: Zero is returned if the function is successful; otherwise, an error number is returned (not in errno).

Error	Description
EAGAIN	Insufficient resources to create another thread, or a system-imposed limit on the number of threads was encountered.
EINVAL	Invalid settings in attr.
EPERM	No permission to set the scheduling policy and parameters specified in attr.

The C language syntax of argument 3 is a bit nasty for beginning C programmers. Let's just show what the function for argument 3 looks like:

```
void *
start_routine(void *arg) {
    ...
    return some_ptr;
}
```

The following is perhaps the simplest example of thread creation possible:

```
static void *
my_thread(void *arg) {
    ...                         // thread execution
    return 0;
}

int
main(int argc, char **argv) {
    pthread_t tid;              // Thread   ID
    int rc;

    rc = pthread_create(&tid,0,my_thread,0);
    assert(!rc);
```

This example does not use thread attributes (argument 2 is zero). We also don't care about the value passed into my_thread(), so argument 4 is provided a zero. Argument 3 simply needs to tell the system call what function to execute. The value of rc will be zero if the thread is successfully created (tested by the assert(3) macro).

51

At this point, the main thread and the function my_thread() execute in parallel. Since there is only one CPU on the Raspberry Pi, only one executes at any instant of time. But they both execute concurrently, trading blocks of execution time in a preemptive manner. Each, of course, runs using its own stack.

Thread my_thread() terminates gracefully, by returning.

pthread_attr_t

There are several thread attributes that can be fetched and set. You'll look only at perhaps the most important attribute (stack size) to keep this crash course brief. For the full list of attributes and functions, you can view the man pages for it:

```
$ man pthread_attr_init
```

To initialize a new attribute, or to release a previously initialized pthread attribute, use this pair of routines:

```
int pthread_attr_init(pthread_attr_t *attr);
int pthread_attr_destroy(pthread_attr_t *attr);
```

> attr: Address of the pthread_attr_t variable to initialize/ destroy
>
> returns: Zero upon success, or an error code when it fails (not in errno)

Error	Description
ENOMEM	Insufficient resources (memory)

The Linux implementation of pthread_attr_init(3) may never return the ENOMEM error, but other Unix platforms might.

The following is a simple example of creating and destroying an attribute object:

```
pthread_attr_t attr;

pthread_attr_init(&attr);     // Initialize attr
...
pthread_attr_destroy(&attr); // Destroy attr
```

Perhaps one of the most important attributes of a thread is the stack size attribute:

```
int pthread_attr_setstacksize(
  pthread_attr_t *attr,
  size_t stacksize
);
```

```
int pthread_attr_getstacksize(
  pthread_attr_t *attr,
  size_t *stacksize
);
```

> attr: The pointer to the attribute to fetch a value from, or to establish an attribute in.
>
> stacksize: This is a stack size value when setting the attribute, and a pointer to the receiving size_t variable when fetching the stack size.
>
> returns: Returns zero if the call is successful; otherwise, returns an error number (not in errno).

The following error is possible for pthread_attr_setstacksize(3):

Error	Description
EINVAL	The stack size is less than PTHREAD_STACK_MIN (16,384) bytes.

The Linux man page further states:

> *On some systems, pthread_attr_setstacksize() can fail with the error EINVAL if stack size is not a multiple of the system page size.*

The following simple example obtains the system default stack size and increases it by 8 MB:

```
pthread_attr_t          attr;
size_t                  stksiz;

pthread_attr_init(&attr);                   // Initialize attr
pthread_attr_getstacksize (&attr,&stksiz);  // Get stack size
stksiz  += 8 * 1024 * 1024;                 // Add 8 MB
pthread_attr_setstacksize(&attr,stksiz);    // Set stack size
```

The system default is provided by the initialization of attr. Then it is a matter of "getting" a value out of the attr object, and then putting in a new stack size in the call to pthread_attr_setstacksize().

Note that this set of operations has simply prepared the attributes object attr for use in a pthread_create() call. The attribute takes effect in the new thread, when the thread is actually created:

```
pthread_attr_t attr;

...
rc = pthread_create(&tid,&attr,my_thread,0);
```

pthread_join(3)

In the earlier pthread_create() example, the main program creates my_thread() and starts it executing. At some point, the main program is going to finish and want to exit (or return). If the main program exits before my_thread() completes, the entire process and the threads in it are destroyed, even if they have not completed.

To cause the main program to wait until the thread completes, the function pthread_join(3) is used:

```
int pthread_join(pthread_t thread, void **retval);
```

> thread: Thread ID of the thread to be joined with.

> retval: Pointer to the void * variable to receive the returned value. If you are uninterested in a return value, this argument can be supplied with zero (or NULL).

> returns: The function returns zero when successful; otherwise, an error number is returned (not in errno).

The following example has added pthread_join(3), so that the main program does not exit until my_thread() exits.

```
int
main(int argc,char **argv) {
        pthread_t tid;                          // Thread ID
        void *retval = 0;                       // Returned value pointer
        int rc;

        rc = pthread_create(&tid,0,my_thread,0);
        assert(!rc);
        rc = pthread_join(tid,&retval);         // Wait for my_thread()
        assert(!rc);
        return 0;
}
```

pthread_detach(3)

The function pthread_join(3) causes the caller to wait until the indicated thread returns. Sometimes, however, a thread is created and never checked again. When that thread exits, some of its resources are retained to allow for a join operation on it. If there is never going to be a join, it is better for that thread to be forgotten when it exits and have its resources immediately released.

The pthread_detach(3) function is used to indicate that no join will be performed on the named thread. This way, the named thread becomes configured to release itself automatically, when it exits.

```
int pthread_detach(pthread_t thread);
```

The argument and return values are as follows:

> thread: The thread ID of the thread to be altered, so that it will not wait for a join when it completes. Its resources will be immediately released upon the named thread's termination.

> returns: Zero if the call was successful; otherwise, an error code is returned (not in errno).

Error	Description
EINVAL	Thread is not a joinable thread.
ESRCH	No thread with the ID thread could be found.

The pthread_detach function simply requires the thread ID value as its argument:

```
pthread_t tid;          // Thread ID
int rc;

rc = pthread_create(&tid,0,my_thread,0);
assert(!rc);
pthread_detach(tid);    // No joining with this thread
```

pthread_self(3)

Sometimes it is convenient in a piece of code to find out what the *current* thread ID is. The pthread_self(3) function is the right tool for the job:

```
pthread_t pthread_self(void);
```

An example of its use is shown here:

```
pthread_t tid;

tid = pthread_self();
```

pthread_kill(3)

The pthread_kill(3) function allows the caller to send a signal to another thread. The handling of thread signals is beyond the scope of this text. But there is one very useful application of this function, which you'll examine shortly:

```
#include <signal.h>

int pthread_kill(pthread_t thread, int sig);
```

Notice that the header file for signal.h is needed for the function prototype and the signal definitions.

> thread: This is the thread ID that you want to signal (or test).

> sig: This is the signal that you wish to send. Alternatively, supply zero to test whether the thread exists.

> returns: Returns zero if the call is successful, or an error code (not in errno).

Error	Description
EINVAL	An invalid signal was specified.
ESRCH	No thread with the ID thread could be found.

One useful application of the pthread_kill(3) function is to test whether another thread exists. If the sig argument is supplied with zero, no actual signal is delivered, but the error checking is still performed. If the function returns zero, you know that the thread still *exists*.

But what does it mean when the thread exists? Does it mean that it is still *executing*? Or does it mean that it has not been reclaimed as part of a pthread_join(3), or as a consequence of pthread_detach(3) cleanup?

It turns out that when the thread *exists*, it means that it is still executing. In other words, it *has not returned* from the thread function that was started. If the thread has returned, it is considered to be incapable of receiving a signal.

Based on this, you know that you will get a zero returned when the thread is still executing. When error code ESRCH is returned instead, you know that the thread has completed.

Mutexes

While not strictly a CPU topic, mutexes cannot be separated from a discussion on threads. A *mutex* is a locking device that allows the software designer to stop one or more threads while another is working with a shared resource. In other words, one thread receives exclusive access. This is necessary to facilitate inter-thread communication. I'm simply going to describe the mutex API here, rather than the theory behind the application of mutexes.

pthread_mutex_create(3)

A mutex is initialized with the system call to pthread_mutex_init(3):

```
int pthread_mutex_init(
    pthread_mutex_t           *mutex,
    const pthread_mutexattr_t *attr
);
```

mutex: A pointer to a `pthread_mutex_t` object, to be initialized.

attr: A pointer to a `pthread_mutexattr_t` object, describing mutex options. Supply zero (or `NULL`), if you can accept the defaults.

returns: Returns zero if the call is successful; otherwise, returns an error code (not in `errno`).

Error	Description
EAGAIN	The system lacks the necessary resources (other than memory) to initialize another mutex.
ENOMEM	Insufficient memory exists to initialize the mutex.
EPERM	The caller does not have the privilege to perform the operation.
EBUSY	The implementation has detected an attempt to reinitialize the object referenced by mutex, a previously initialized, but not yet destroyed, mutex.
EINVAL	The value specified by attr is invalid.

An example of mutex initialization is provided here:

```
pthread_mutex_t mutex;
int rc;

rc = pthread_mutex_init(&mutex,0);
assert (!rc);
```

pthread_mutex_destroy(3)

When the application no longer needs a mutex, it should use `pthread_mutex_destroy(3)` to release its resources:

```
pthread_mutex_t mutex ;
int rc;

...
rc = pthread_mutex_destroy(&mutex);
assert(!rc);
```

mutex: The address of the mutex to release resources for

returns: Returns zero when successful, or an error code when it fails (not in `errno`)

Error	Description
EBUSY	Mutex is locked or in use in conjunction with a pthread_cond_wait(3) or pthread_cond_timedwait(3).
EINVAL	The value specified by mutex is invalid.

pthread_mutex_lock(3)

When a thread needs exclusive access to a resource, it must lock the resource's mutex. As long as the cooperating threads follow the same procedure of locking first, they cannot both access the shared object at the same time.

```
int pthread_mutex_lock(pthread_mutex_t *mutex);
```

> mutex: A pointer to the mutex to lock.
>
> returns: Returns zero if the mutex was successfully locked; otherwise, an error code is returned (not in errno).

Error	Description
EINVAL	The mutex was created with the protocol attribute having the value PTHREAD_PRIO_PROTECT, and the calling thread's priority is higher than the mutex's current priority ceiling. Or the value specified by the mutex does not refer to an initialized mutex object.
EAGAIN	Maximum number of recursive locks for mutex has been exceeded.
EDEADLK	The current thread already owns the mutex.

The following shows the function being called:

```
pthread_mutex_t mutex;
int rc;

...
rc = pthread_mutex_lock(&mutex);
```

pthread_mutex_unlock(3)

When exclusive access to a resource is no longer required, the mutex is unlocked:

```
int pthread_mutex_unlock(pthread_mutex_t *mutex);
```

> mutex: A pointer to the mutex to be unlocked.
>
> returns: Returns zero if the mutex was unlocked successfully; otherwise, an error code is returned (not in errno).

Error	Description
EINVAL	The value specified by mutex does not refer to an initialized mutex object.
EPERM	The current thread does not own the mutex.

A simple example of unlocking a mutex is provided here:

```
pthread_mutex_t mutex;
int rc;

...
rc = pthread_mutex_unlock(&mutex);
```

Condition Variables

Sometimes mutexes alone are not enough for efficient scheduling of CPU between different threads. Mutexes and condition variables are often used together to facilitate inter-thread communication. Some beginners might struggle with this concept, if they are seeing it for the first time.

Why do we need condition variables when we have mutexes?

Consider what is necessary in building a software queue that can hold a maximum of eight items. Before we can queue something, we need to first see if the queue is full. But we cannot test that until we have the queue locked—otherwise, another thread could be changing things under our own noses.

So we lock the queue but find that it is full. What do we do now? Do we simply unlock and try again? This works but it wastes CPU resources. Wouldn't it be better if we had some way of being alerted when the queue was no longer full?

The condition variable works in concert with a mutex and a "signal" (of sorts). In pseudo code terms, a program trying to queue an item on a queue would perform the following steps:

1. Lock the mutex. We cannot examine anything in the queue until we lock it.

2. Check the queue's capacity. Can we place a new item in it? If so:

   a. Place the new item in the queue.

   b. Unlock and exit.

3. If the queue is full, the following steps are performed:

   a. Using a condition variable, "wait" on it, with the associated mutex.

   b. When control returns from the wait, return to step 2.

How does the condition variable help us? Consider the following steps:

1. The mutex is locked (1).

2. The wait is performed (3a). This causes the kernel to do the following:

   a. Put the calling thread to sleep (put on a wait queue)

   b. Unlock the mutex that was locked in step 1

Unlocking of the mutex in step 2b is necessary so that another thread can do something with the queue (hopefully, take an entry from the queue so that it is no longer full). If the mutex remained locked, no thread would be able to move.

At some future point in time, another thread will do the following:

1. Lock the mutex

2. Find entries in the queue (it was currently full), and pull one item out of it

3. Unlock the mutex

4. Signal the condition variable that the "waiter" is using, so that it can wake up

The waiting thread then awakens:

1. The kernel makes the "waiting" thread ready.

2. The mutex is successfully relocked.

Once that thread awakens with the mutex locked, it can recheck the queue to see whether there is room to queue an item. Notice that *the thread is awakened only when it has already reacquired the mutex lock*. This is why condition variables are paired with a mutex in their use.

pthread_cond_init(3)

Like any other object, a condition variable needs to be initialized:

```
int pthread_cond_init(
  pthread_cond_t        *cond,
  const pthread_condattr_t  *attr
);
```

cond: A pointer to the pthread_cond_t structure to be initialized.

attr: A pointer to a cond variable attribute if one is provided, or supply zero (or NULL).

returns: Zero is returned if the call is successful; otherwise, an error code is returned (not in errno).

Error	Description
EAGAIN	The system lacked the necessary resources.
ENOMEM	Insufficient memory exists to initialize the condition variable.
EBUSY	The implementation has detected an attempt to reinitialize the object referenced by cond, a previously initialized, but not yet destroyed, condition variable.
EINVAL	The value specified by attr is invalid.

pthread_cond_destroy(3)

When a condition (cond) variable is no longer required, its resources should be released with the following call:

```
int pthread_cond_destroy(pthread_cond_t *cond);
```

> cond: Condition variable to be released.

> returns: Zero if the call was successful; otherwise, returns an error code (not in errno).

Error	Description
EBUSY	Detected an attempt to destroy the object referenced by cond while it is referenced by pthread_cond_wait() or pthread_cond_timedwait() in another thread.
EINVAL	The value specified by cond is invalid.

pthread_cond_wait(3)

This function is one-half of the queue solution. The pthread_cond_wait(3) function is called with the mutex already locked. The kernel will then put the calling thread to sleep (on the wait queue) to release the CPU, while at the same time unlocking the mutex. The calling thread remains blocked until the condition variable cond is signaled in some way (more about that later).

When the thread is awakened by the kernel, the system call returns with the mutex locked. At this point, the thread can check the application condition (like queue length) and then proceed if things are favorable, or call pthread_cond_wait(3) again to wait further.

```
int pthread_cond_wait(
  pthread_cond_t *cond,
  pthread_mutex_t *mutex
);
```

cond: Pointer to the condition variable to be used for the wake-up call.

mutex: Pointer to the mutex to be associated with the condition variable.

returns: Returns zero upon success; otherwise, an error code is returned (not in errno).

Error	Description
EINVAL	The value specified by cond, mutex is invalid. Or different mutexes were supplied for concurrent pthread_cond_timedwait() or pthread_cond_wait() operations on the same condition variable.
EPERM	The mutex was not owned by the current thread at the time of the call.

The following code snippet shows how a queuing function would use this. (Initialization of mutex and cond is assumed.)

```
pthread_mutex_t mutex;
pthread_cond_t cond;

...
pthread_mutex_lock(&mutex);

while ( queue.length >= max_length )
    pthread_cond_wait(&cond,&mutex);

// queue the item
...
pthread_mutex_unlock(&mutex);
```

The while loop retries the test to see whether the queue is "not full." The while loop is necessary when multiple threads are inserting into the queue. Depending on timing, another thread could beat the current thread to queuing an item, making the queue full again.

pthread_cond_signal(3)

When an item is taken off the queue, a mechanism needs to wake up the thread attempting to put one entry into the full queue. One wake-up option is the pthread_cond_signal(3) system call:

```
int pthread_cond_signal(pthread_cond_t *cond);
```

cond: A pointer to the condition variable used to signal one thread

returns: Returns zero if the function call was successful; otherwise, an error number is returned (not in errno).

Error	Description
EINVAL	The value cond does not refer to an initialized condition variable.

It is *not* an error if no other thread is waiting. This function does, however, wake up one waiting thread, if one or more are waiting on the specified condition variable.

This call is preferred for *performance* reasons if signaling one thread will "work." When there are special conditions whereby some threads may succeed and others would not, you need a *broadcast* call instead. When it can be used, waking *one* thread saves CPU cycles.

pthread_cond_broadcast(3)

This is the broadcast variant of pthread_cond_signal(3). If multiple waiters have different tests, a broadcast should be used to allow *all* waiters to wake up and consider the conditions found.

```
int pthread_cond_broadcast(pthread_cond_t *cond);
```

cond: A pointer to the condition variable to be *signaled*, waking *all* waiting threads.

returns: Zero is returned when the call is successful; otherwise, an error number is returned (not in errno).

Error	Description
EINVAL	The value cond does not refer to an initialized condition variable.

It is *not* an error to broadcast when there are no waiters.

## CHAPTER 6

USB

The USB port has become ubiquitous in the digital world, allowing the use of a large choice of peripherals. The Model B Raspberry Pi supports two USB 2 ports, and the Model A just one.

This chapter briefly examines some power considerations associated with USB support and powered hubs. The remainder of this chapter examines the device driver interface available to the Raspbian Linux developer. Figure 6-1 serves as a chapter reference schematic of the Raspberry USB interface.

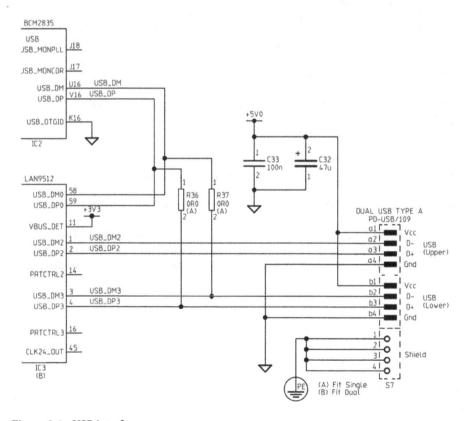

Figure 6-1. *USB interface*

Power

Early models of the Raspberry Pi limited each USB port to 100 mA because of the polyfuses included. Revision 2.0 models did away with these, leaving you with more options.

Even with the polyfuses removed, the end user should remember that the USB ports are powered by the input to the Raspberry Pi PCB. This is supplied through fuse F3 (see Figure 4-3, shown previously in Chapter 2). This limits the maximum USB current to 500 mA for the Model A (which is the limit for one USB port anyway) and 300 mA for the Model B. Exceeding these limits could cause fuse F3 to blow.

■ **Note**   Wireless USB adapters consume between 350 mA and 500 mA.

Powered Hubs

Whether you have a Model A or Model B Raspberry Pi, you'll want to use a powered USB hub for high-current peripherals. This is particularly true for wireless network adapters, since they often require up to 500 mA.

A USB hub requires coordination with the Linux kernel and thus requires Raspbian Linux driver support. A number of hubs have been reported not to work. The following web page is a good resource listing hubs that are known work with Raspbian Linux:

```
http://elinux.org/RPi_Powered_USB_Hubs
```

With the powered USB hub plugged in, you can list the USB devices that have registered with the kernel by using the lsusb command:

```
# lsusb
Bus 001 Device 001: ID 1d6b:0002 Linux Foundation 2.0 root hub
Bus 001 Device 002: ID 0424:9512 Standard Microsystems Corp.
Bus 001 Device 003: ID 0424:ec00 Standard Microsystems Corp.
Bus 001 Device 004: ID 0451:2077 Texas Instruments, Inc. TUSB2077 Hub
```

The first three listed are the usual suspects from the Pi's own hardware. The last line shows that a TUSB2077 Hub has been registered. Figure 6-2 shows my Belkin USB hub on a busy workbench. If your hub fails to appear in this report, it likely means that there is no driver support for it.

Figure 6-2. *A powered USB hub*

USB API Support

USB devices are normally supported by device drivers and appear as generic peripherals like keyboards, mice, or storage. The USB Boarduino is a little different, using the FTDI chipset, and supported by a driver.

Once the Boarduino is plugged in, the lsusb command lists it, thanks to the FTDI chipset driver:

```
$ lsusb
...
Bus 001 Device 008: ID 0403:6001 Future Technology Devices \
        International, Ltd FT232 USB-Serial (UART) IC
```

The supporting driver makes the Boarduino available as a serial device:

```
$ ls -l /dev/ttyUSB0
crw-rw—T 1 root dialout 188, 0 Dec 31 1969 /dev/ttyUSB0
```

The serial device support allows the AVR device to be programmed by avrdude. A Raspberry Pi application can also communicate with the AVR device's application. If you want to use network-like packets, the SLIP serial protocol, for example, can be used to communicate over that link. The "Serial API" section of Chapter 9 covers the Linux API for serial communications.

libusb

Although USB devices are supported by drivers and appear as generic devices, in some situations a user space program needs to communicate with specialized hardware. While Raspbian Linux has libusb installed, the developer will want to install the developer package for it:

```
# apt-get install libusb-dev
```

The USB API is fairly large, complex and beyond the scope of this text. But the curious developer can read more about the libusb API at the website:

http://libusb.sourceforge.net/doc/index.html

In this chapter, you'll examine just the beginnings of a libusb program, so that you can get a flavor of how the API works.

Include Files

The main include file for Raspbian libusb support is as follows:

#include <usb.h>

The next few pages show a simple USB program, which enumerates USB buses and devices. Once a device is located, an attempt is made to "claim" it and then release it (it will print CLAIMED if successful). However, when all of your USB devices are fully supported by drivers, none will be claimed. This list can be checked against the lsusb command output.

The next example program was run on a Raspberry Pi with the following USB devices reported by lsusb:

```
$ lsusb
Bus 001 Device 002: ID 0424:9512 Standard Microsystems Corp.
Bus 001 Device 001: ID 1d6b:0002 Linux Foundation 2.0 root hub
Bus 001 Device 003: ID 0424:ec00 Standard Microsystems Corp.
Bus 001 Device 004: ID 05ac:1002 Apple, Inc. Extended Keyboard Hub [Mitsumi]
Bus 001 Device 005: ID 0451:2077 Texas Instruments, Inc. TUSB2077 Hub
Bus 001 Device 006: ID 05ac:0204 Apple, Inc.
Bus 001 Device 007: ID 045e:0040 Microsoft Corp. Wheel Mouse Optical
```

The example program was compiled by the provided make file in the libusb subdirectory and invoked as follows:

```
$ ./tusb
Device: 007 045e:0040    class 0.0 protocol 0 device 768, manuf 1, serial 0
   0.0.0 class 3
Device: 006 05ac:0204    class 0.0 protocol 0 device 290, manuf 1, serial 0
   0.0.0 class 3
   0.1.0 class 3
Device: 005 0451:2077    class 9.0 protocol 0 device 256, manuf 0, serial 0
   0.0.0 class 9
Device: 004 05ac:1002    class 9.0 protocol 0 device 290, manuf 1, serial 0
   0.0.0 class 9
Device: 003 0424:ec00    class 255.0 protocol 1 device 512, manuf 0, serial 0
   0.0.0 class 255
```

```
Device: 002 0424:9512     class 9.0 protocol 2 device 512, manuf 0, serial 0
   0.0.0 class 9
   0.0.1 class 9
Device: 001 1d6b:0002     class 9.0 protocol 1 device 774, manuf 3, serial 1
   0.0.0 class 9
```

These are easily compared by noting the device name, such as 007, which is reported by lsusb to be the Microsoft mouse.

```
1   /*********************************************************************
2    * tusb.c - Scan list of USB devices and test claim/release.
3    *********************************************************************/
4
5   #include <stdio.h>
6   #include <stdlib.h>
7   #include <errno.h>
8   #include <usb.h>
9   #include <assert.h>
10
11  /*********************************************************************
12   * See http://libusb.sourceforge.net/doc/index.html for API
13   *********************************************************************/
14
15  int
16  main(int argc, char **argv) {
17      struct usb_bus *busses, *bus;
18      struct usb_device *dev;
19      struct usb_device_descriptor *desc;
20      usb_dev_handle *hdev;
21      int cx, ix, ax, rc;
22
23      usb_init();
24      usb_find_busses();
25      usb_find_devices();
26
27      busses = usb_get_busses();
28
29      for ( bus=busses; bus; bus = bus->next ) {
30          for ( dev=bus->devices; dev; dev = dev->next ) {
31              desc = &dev->descriptor;
32
33              printf("Device: %s %04x:%04x ",
34                  dev->filename,
35                  desc->idVendor,
36                  desc->idProduct);
37              printf(" class %u.%d protocol %u",
38                  desc->bDeviceClass,
39                  desc->bDeviceSubClass,
```

```
40                      desc->bDeviceProtocol);
41              printf(" device %u, manuf %u, serial %u\n",
42                      desc->bcdDevice,
43                      desc->iManufacturer,
44                      desc->iSerial Number);
45
46              hdev = usb_open(dev);
47              assert(hdev);
48
49              rc = usb_claim_interface(hdev,0);
50              if ( !rc ) {
51                      puts("  CLAIMED..");
52                      rc = usb_release_interface(hdev, 0);
53                      puts("  RELEASED..");
54                      assert(!rc);
55              }
56              usb_close(hdev);
57
58              /* Configurations */
59              for ( cx=0; cx <dev->descriptor.bNumConfigurations;
                ++cx ) {
60                      /* Interfaces */
61                      for ( ix=0; ix < dev->config[cx].bNumInterfaces;
                        ++ix ) {
62                              /* Alternates */
63                              for ( ax=0; ax < dev->config[cx].interface[ix].
                                num_altsetting;
                                        ++ax ) {
64                                      printf("  %d.%d.%d class %u\n",
65                                          cx,ix,ax,
66                                          dev->config[cx].interface[ix].
                                                altsetting[ax].bInterfaceClass);
67                              }
68                      }
69              }
70      }
71      }
72
73      return 0;
74  }
75
76  /* End tusb.c */
```

CHAPTER 7

Ethernet

Networking has become an important part of everyday life, whether wireless or by wire. Having a network adapter on your Raspberry Pi allows you to connect to it and do things on it from the comfort of your desktop or laptop computer. It also allows your application on the Pi to reach out to the outside world. Even when the Raspberry Pi is deployed as part of an embedded project, the network interface continues to be important. Remote logging and control are just two examples.

Wired Ethernet

The standard Raspbian SD card image provides a wired network connection, using DHCP to automatically assign an IP address to it. If you are using the HDMI output and keyboard devices to do work on the Pi, the dynamically assigned IP address is not a bother. But if you would like to eliminate the attached display and keyboard, connecting over the network is attractive. The only problem is the potentially changing IP address. (DHCP will not always use a different IP address, since the address is leased for a time). It is difficult to contact your Raspberry Pi from a laptop until you know its IP address. As covered in Chapter 1 of *Raspberry Pi System Software Reference* (Apress, 2014), you can use the nmap command to scan for it, but this is inconvenient:

```
$ sudo nmap -sP 192.168.0.1-254

Starting Nmap 6.25 (http://nmap.org) at 2013-04-14 19:12 EDT
. . .
Nmap scan report for mac (192.168.0.129)
Host is up.
Nmap scan report for rasp (192.168.0.132)
Host is up (0.00071s latency).
MAC Address: B8:27:EB:2B:69:E8 ( Raspberry Pi Foundation )
Nmap done : 254 IP addresses (6 hosts up) scanned in 6.01 seconds
$
```

If you use your Pi at school or away from your own premises, using DHCP may still be the best option for you. If you are plugging it into different networks as you travel, DHCP sets up your IP address properly and *takes care of the name server configuration*. However, if you are using your unit at home, or your school can assign you a valid IP address to use, a static IP address simplifies access.

■ **Note**   Be sure to get approval and an IP address assigned to prevent network conflicts.

/etc/network/interfaces

As supplied by the standard Raspbian image, the /etc/network/interfaces file looks
like this:

```
$ cat /etc/network/interfaces
auto lo

iface lo inet loopback
iface eth0 inet dhcp

allow-hotplug wlan0
iface wlan0 inet manual
wpa-roam/etc/wpa_supplicant/wpa_supplicant.conf
iface default inet dhcp
$
```

The wired Ethernet interface (Model B) is named eth0. The line starting with
iface eth0 indicates that your network interface eth0 is using DHCP. If this is what
you want, leave it as is.

Changing to Static IP

If you haven't booted up your Raspberry Pi with the network cable plugged in, now is
a good time to do that. This may save you time later, when we review the name server
settings.

Next, before you start changing it, save a backup of the /etc/network/interfaces
file in case you want to change it back:

```
$ sudo -i
# cd /etc/network
# cp interfaces interfaces.bak
```

Next, edit the line in /etc/network/interfaces that begins with iface eth0 so that
it reads like the following:

```
iface eth0 inet static
    address     192.168.0.177
    gateway     192.168.0.1
    netmask     255.255.255.0
    network     192.168.0.0
    broadcast   192.168.0.255
```

In this example, we have established a fixed IP address of 192.168.0.177, along with the appropriate settings for gateway, netmask, network, and broadcast address. If the network is not your own, get a network administrator to help you with the correct values to use.

There is one other file that needs to be checked and potentially edited:

```
$ cat /etc/resolv.conf
domain myfastisp.net
search myfastisp.net
nameserver 192.168.0.1
```

If you've booted up your Raspberry Pi previously while it was using DHCP (with network cable plugged in), these values may already be suitably configured. Otherwise, you'll need to edit them to get the name service to work. In this example, the Internet Service Provider is myfastisp.net, and name service requests are forwarded through the firewall router at 192.168.0.1.

Test Static IP Address

Once you have configured things, the simplest thing to do is to reboot your Raspberry Pi to make the new settings take effect (use sudo /sbin/reboot or sudo /sbin/shutdown -r now).

Once you've rebooted and logged in, check your IP address:

```
$ ifconfig eth0
eth0 Link encap : Ethernet HWaddr b8:27:eb:2b:69:e9
     inet addr:192.168.0.177   Bcast: 192.168.0.255   Mask: 255.255.255.0
     UP BROADCAST RUNNING MULTICAST MTU: 1500 Metric: 1
     RX packets: 1046 errors: 0 dropped : 3 overruns: 0 frame: 0
     TX packets: 757 errors: 0 dropped: 0 over runs : 0 carrier: 0
     collisions:0 txqueuelen :1000
     RX bytes: 74312 (72.5 KiB) TX bytes: 86127 (84.1 KiB)
```

In the preceding example, the inet addr matches our configured static IP address. Let's now check that the names are resolving. Normally, I would recommend nslookup or dig for this, but neither comes preinstalled on Raspbian. So let's just use ping:

```
$ ping -c1 google.com
PING google.com (74.125.226.4) 56 (84) bytes of data.
64 bytes from yyz06s05-in-f4.1e100.net (74.125.226.4): . . .

--- google.com ping statistics ---
1 packets transmitted, 1 received, 0% packet loss, time 0ms
rtt min/avg/max/mdev = 11.933/11.933/11.933/0.000 ms
$
```

In this example, we see that google.com was looked up and translated to the IP address 74.125.226.4. From this, we conclude that the name service is working. The -c1 option on the ping command line causes only one ping to be performed. Otherwise, ping will keep trying, and you may need to ^C to interrupt its execution.

If the name google.com does not resolve, you'll need to troubleshoot /etc/resolv.conf. As a last resort, you might switch back to using DHCP (interfaces.bak) and reboot. If the /etc/resolv.conf file is updated with new parameters, you might try again.

USB Adapters

If you have a USB Ethernet adapter (non-wireless), you can set up networking for that also. The following line added to /etc/network/interfaces will cause it to use DHCP:

```
iface usb0 inet dhcp
```

For a fixed usb0 IP address, configure as we did earlier (for eth0). For example:

```
iface usb0 inet static
   address   192.168.0.178
   gateway   192.168.0.1
   netmask   255.255.255.0
   network   192.168.0.0
   broadcast 192.168.0.255
```

This provides interface usb0 with a fixed address of 192.168.0.178.

/etc/hosts File

If you have a static IP address for your Raspberry Pi, why not update your Linux, OS X, or Windows hosts file (typically, C:\Windows\system32\drivers\etc\hosts) with a hostname for it? For example, your hosts file could have the following line added:

```
$ cat /etc/hosts
. . .
192.168.0.177 rasp raspi rpi pi # My Raspberry Pi
```

Now you can use a hostname of rasp, raspi, rpi, or pi to access your Raspberry Pi on the network.

Wireless Ethernet

If you haven't already done so, review the "Powered Hubs" section of Chapter 6. Wi-Fi adapters can require 350 mA to 500 mA of current draw.

The following web page lists good information about the various brands of Wi-Fi adapters available and their level of support:

http://elinux.org/RPi_USB_Wi-Fi_Adapters

I have a NetGear WN111(v2) RangeMax Next Wireless adapter available. Apparently, this adapter uses one of the following chips:

- Atheros AR9170

- Atheros AR9101

Since the AR9170 shows up in the supported list for the D-Link DWA-160, there is a reasonable chance of driver support for it. After plugging it into the powered USB hub and rebooting, the console log shows that it is being "*seen*":

```
$ dmesg
. . .
[3.867883] usb 1_1.3.2: New USB device found, idVendor=0846, idProduct=9001
[3.893138] usb 1_1.3.2: New USB device strings: Mfr=16, Product=32,
SerialNumber=
[3.923115] usb 1_1.3.2: Product: USB2.0 WLAN
[3.930064] usb 1_1.3.2: Manufacturer : ATHER
[3.963095] usb 1_1.3.2: SerialNumber : 12345
[4.393875] cfg80211: Calling CRDA to update world regulatory domain
[4.663403] usb 1_1.3.2: reset full_speed USB device number 5 using dwc_otg
[4.953470] usbcore: registered new interface driver carl9170
[6.687035] usb 1_1.3.2: firmware not found.
[7.703098] usb 1_1.3.2: kill pending tx urbs.
```

But there is a troubling error message: "firmware not found." Also visible in the log, we see that the driver is named carl9170. Further research reveals that it also requires a firmware file named carl9170-1.fw. While this file is available from other sources, the simplest way to install this file is to install it from Raspbian sources:

```
$ sudo apt-get install firmware-linux
```

The firmware file being sought and installed is as follows:

```
$ ls -l /lib/firmware/carl9170-1.fw
-rw-r--r--1 root root 13388 Jan 14 17:04 /lib/firmware/carl9170-1.fw
```

Rebooting again, the missing firmware message is gone. The lsusb report also confirms the device is ready:

```
# lsusb
Bus 001 Device 001: ID 1d6b :0002 Linux Foundation 2.0 root hub
Bus 001 Device 002: ID 0424:9512 Standard Microsystems Corp.
Bus 001 Device 003: ID 0424: ec00 Standard Microsystems Corp.
Bus 001 Device 004: ID 0451:2077 Texas Instruments, Inc. TUSB2077 Hub
Bus 001 Device 005: ID 0846:9001 NetGear, Inc. WN111(v2) RangeMax \
   Next Wireless [Atheros AR9170+AR9101]
#
```

The hardware driver support is now in place. The device now needs network configuration.

Configuration

You could edit the configuration files by hand if you knew all the possible keywords necessary for your particular wireless authentication protocol. The following Linux raspberrypi 3.2.27+ files are involved:

Pathname	Description
/etc/network/interfaces	Main configuration file for networks
/etc/wpa_supplicant/wpa_supplicant.conf	Authentication information

You'll find a variety of advice on how to configure these on the Internet. But the quickest path to success is to just use the wpa_gui dialog box from the Raspberry Pi desktop. Once you've done it this way, directly editing the configuration files can be performed later if you need to tweak it further.

Figure 7-1 shows how to locate the wpa_gui dialog box from your Pi desktop. Once wpa_gui is started, click the Manage Networks tab, shown in Figure 7-2. If you've made prior attempts at configuring wlan0, delete them all from this menu. Then click the Scan button at the bottom right.

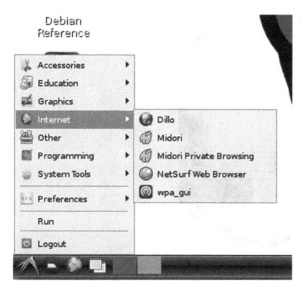

Figure 7-1. *wpa_gui dialog box*

Figure 7-2. *The Manage Networks tab*

After clicking Scan, your wireless network should eventually appear in the scan list, as shown in Figure 7-3.

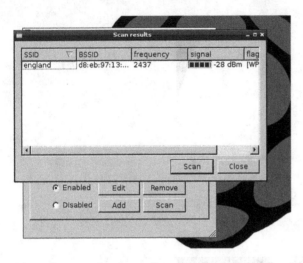

Figure 7-3. *Results of a wireless network scan*

Double-click the line representing your network. This brings up a new dialog box that allows you to fill in the remaining authentication parameters:

Parameter	Example
Authentication	WPA-Personal (PSK)
Encryption	CCMP
PSK	Pass phrase

Enter settings that apply to your network. After completing the data input, click the Add button. As you exit the dialog box, *be sure to select Save Configuration from the File menu.*

■ **Caution** Don't forget to pull down Save Configuration from the File menu before you exit the setup application. This is easily forgotten, and no reminder of unsaved changes is provided.

After saving the new Wi-Fi configuration, reboot. After the Pi comes back up, log in and check the network interfaces. Look for interface wlan0:

```
$ ifconfig
. . .
wlan0 Link encap: Ethernet HWaddr 00:22:3f:8d: 78: f9
        inet addr:192.168.0.61 Bcast:192.168.0.255 Mask:255.255.255.0
        UP BROADCAST RUNNING MULTICAST MTU: 1500 Metric: 1
        RX packets: 10514 errors: 0 dropped: 0 overruns: 0 frame : 0
        TX packets: 121 errors: 0 dropped : 0 over runs: 0 carrier: 0
        collisions:0 txqueuelen:1000
        RX bytes: 767287 (749.3 KiB) TX bytes: 9188 (8.9 KiB)
```

The preceding example shows that the wlan0 is available and has a DHCP-assigned IP address. You can now ping or ssh to this access point.

■ ■ ■

## CHAPTER 8

SD Card Storage

The file system is central to the Unix system design, from which Linux borrows. The necessary mass storage requirements have traditionally been fulfilled through hard disk subsystems. However, as Linux hosts become as small as cell phones, flash memory technology has replaced the bulky mechanical drive.

SD Card Media

The standard SD card is 32 mm long, 24 mm wide, and 2.1 mm thick. Figure 8-1 illustrates the connections available on the underside of the SD card. The schematic excerpt shown later will document how the connections are made to this media.

Figure 8-1. *SD card pinout*

SD Card Interface

In the Raspberry Pi, the SD card is interfaced to the SoC through GPIO pins 46 through 53, seen in Figure 8-2. The SoC senses the insertion of an SD card through the closing of a socket switch (pins 10 and 11 of the socket). Thus GPIO 47 is brought to ground potential when the socket is occupied.

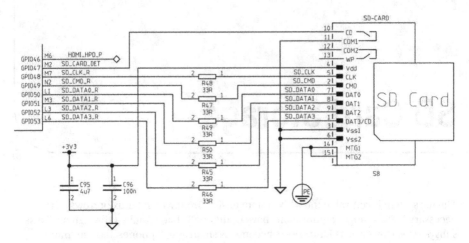

Figure 8-2. *SD card circuit*

Looking at the wiring in Figure 8-2, it might be assumed that all data transfers are 4 bits wide (GPIO 50 through GPIO 53). However, as the following sections will describe, this depends on the SD card media used.

SD Card Basics

The SD card includes an internal controller, also known as a Flash Storage Processor (FSP). In this configuration, the Linux host merely provides a command and waits for the response. The FSP takes care of all erase, programming, and read operations necessary to complete the command. In this way, Flash card designs are permitted to increase in complexity as new performance and storage densities are implemented.

The SD card manages data with a sector size of 512 bytes. This was intentionally made the same as the IDE magnetic disk drive for compatibility with existing operating systems. Commands issued by the host include a sector address to allow read/writes of one or more sectors.

■ **Note**   Operating systems may use a multiple of the 512-byte sector.

Commands and data are protected by CRC codes in the FSP. The FSP also automatically performs a read after write to verify that the data is written correctly.[21] If the data write is found defective, the FSP automatically corrects it, replacing the physical sector with another if necessary.

The SD card soft error rate is much lower than a magnetic disk drive. In the rare case when errors are discovered, the last line of defense is a correcting ECC, which allows for data recovery. These errors are corrected in the media to prevent future unrecoverable errors. All of this activity is transparent to the host.

Raspbian Block Size

The block size used by the operating system may be a multiple of the media's sector size. To determine the physical block size used under Raspbian, we first discover how the root file system is mounted (the following listing has been trimmed with ellipses):

```
$ mount
/dev/root on/type ext4 (rw, noatime, . . . )
. . .
/dev/mmcblk0p1 on/boot type vfat (rw, relatime , . . . )
$
```

From this we deduce that the device used for the root file system is /dev/root. The pathname given is a symbolic link, so we need to determine the real device pathname:

```
$ ls -dl /dev/root
lrwxrwxrwx 1 root root 9 Jan 12 19:33/dev/root -> mmcblk0p2
$
```

From this, we deduce that the actual device pathname is /dev/mmcblk0p2. The naming convention used tells us the following:

Component	Name	Number	Type
Prefix	/dev/mmcblk		MMC block
Device number	0	0	
Partition number	p2	2	

From the earlier mount command output, notice that the /boot file system was mounted on /dev/mmcblk0p1. (No symbolic link was used in this case.) From this we understand that the /boot file system is from partition 1 of the same SD card device.

Using the root device information, we consult the /sys pseudo file system to find out the physical sector size. Here we supply mmcblk0 as the third-level pathname qualifier to query the device:

```
$ cat /sys/block/mmcblk0/queue/physical_block_size
 512
$ cat /sys/block/mmcblk0/queue/logical_block_size
 512
$
```

The result shown informs us that the Raspbian Linux used in this example uses a block (sector) size of 512 bytes, both physically and logically. This precisely matches the SD card's sector size. Since the /boot file system uses the same physical device as root, this also applies to that partition.

Disk Cache

While we're examining mounted SD card file systems, let's also check the type of device node used:

```
$ ls -l /dev/mmcblk0p?
brw-rw---T 1 root floppy 179, 1 Dec 31 1969  /dev/mmcblk0p1
brw-rw---T 1 root floppy 179, 2 Jan 12 19:33  /dev/mmcblk0p2
$
```

The example output shows a b at the beginning of the brw-rw—T field. This tells us that the disk device is a *block* device as opposed to a *character* device. (The associated character device would show a c instead.) Block devices are important for file systems because they provide a disk cache capability to vastly improve the file system performance. The output shows that both the root (partition 2) and the /boot (partition 1) file systems are mounted using block devices.

Capacities and Performance

SD cards allow a configurable data bus width within limits of the media. All SD cards start with one data bit line until the capabilities of the memory card are known:

> *The SD bus allows dynamic configuration of the number of data lines. After power-up, by default, the SD card will use only DAT0 for data transfer. After initialization, the host can change the bus width (number of active data lines). This feature allows [an] easy trade-off between hardware cost and system performance.*[18]

After the capabilities of the media are known, the data bus can be expanded under software control, as supported. Given that SD cards with memory capacities up to 2 GB operate with a 1-bit data bus, it is highly desirable to use a 4 GB or larger card on the Raspberry Pi, even if the extra storage is not required. More-advanced cards also offer greater transfer speeds by use of higher data clock rates.

Table 8-1 summarizes SD card capabilities.[19]

Table 8-1. *SD Card Capabilities*

Standard	Description	Greater Than	Up To	Data Bus
SDSC	Standard capacity	0	2 GB	1-bit
SDHC	High capacity	2 GB	32 GB	4-bit
SDXC	Extended capacity	32 GB	2 TB	4-bit

Transfer Modes

There are three basic data transfer modes used by SD cards:[18]

- SPI Bus mode
- 1-bit SD mode
- 4-bit SD mode

SPI Bus Mode

The SPI Bus mode is used mainly by consumer electronics using small microcontrollers supporting the SPI bus. Examining Table 8-2 reveals that data is transmitted 1 bit at a time in this mode (pin 2 or 7).

Table 8-2. *SPI Bus Mode*

Pin	Name	I/O	Logic	Description	SPI
1	nCS	I	PP	Card select (negative true)	CS
2	DI	I	PP	Data in	MOSI
3	VSS	S	S	Ground	
4	VDD	S	S	Power	
5	CLK	I	PP	Clock	SCLK
6	VSS	S	S	Ground	
7	DO	O	PP	Data out	MISO
8	NC			Memory cards	
	nIRQ	O	OD	Interrupt on SDIO cards	
9	NC			Not connected	

The various SD card connections are used in different ways, as documented by the Table 8-2 mnemonics in the columns I/O and Logic. Table 8-3 is a legend for these and also applies to later Tables 10-4 and 10-5.

Table 8-3. *Legend for I/O and Logic*

Notation	Meaning	Notes
I	Input	Relative to card
O	Output	
I/O	Input or output	
PP	Push/pull logic	
OD	Open drain	
S	Power supply	
NC	Not connected	Or logic high

1-bit SD Mode

Table 8-4 lists the pins and functions of the SD card when it is in 1-bit SD mode. The data traverses pin 7 (DAT0) while the clock is supplied on pin 5. Pin 2 is used to send commands and receive responses. This mode uses a proprietary transfer format.

Table 8-4. *1-bit SD Mode*

Pin	Name	I/O	Logic	Description
1	NC			No connection
2	CMD	I/O	PP/OD	Command/response
3	VSS	S	S	Ground
4	VDD	S	S	Power
5	CLK	I	PP	Clock
6	VSS	S	S	Ground
7	DAT0	I/O	PP	Data 0
8	NC	NC		Memory cards
	nIRQ	O	OD	SDIO cards
9	NC			No connection

4-bit SD Mode

This is the mode used when the data bus width is more than a single bit and supported by SDHC and SDXC cards. Higher data clock rates also improve transfer rates. Table 8-5 lists the pin assignments.

Table 8-5. *4-bit SD Mode*

Pin	Name	I/O	Logic	Description
1	DAT3	I/O	PP	Data 3
2	CMD	I/O	PP/OD	Command/response
3	VSS	S	S	Ground
4	VDD	S	S	Power
5	CLK	I	PP	Clock
6	VSS	S	S	Ground
7	DAT0	I/O	PP	Data 0
8	DAT1	I/O	PP	Data 1
	nIRQ	O	OD	SDIO cards share with interrupt
9	DAT2	I/O	PP	Data 2

Wear Leveling

Unfortunately, Flash memory is subject to *wear* for each *write* operation performed (as each write requires erasing and programming a block of data). The design of Flash memory requires that a large block of memory be erased and rewritten, even if a single sector has changed value. For this reason, wear leveling is used as a technique to extend the life of the media. Wear leveling extends life by moving data to different physical blocks while retaining the same logical address.

■ **Note**   ScanDisk calls the block of Flash memory being erased and rewritten a *zone*.

Some cards use wear leveling.[18] Indeed the SanDisk company indicates that their products do use wear leveling.[20] However, the type of wear leveling supported by SanDisk is limited to zones within the media. Each SanDisk zone has 3% extra capacity, from which writes can be wear leveled within. If the zone size is 4 MB and is overprovisioned by 3%, this leaves about 245 spare sectors within each zone. Thus each 4 MB zone holds 8,192 active sectors at any given instant, rotated among 245 spares.

■ **Note** SanDisk indicates that the 4 MB zones may change with future memory capacities.

Other manufacturers may not implement wear leveling at all or use a lower level of overprovisioning. Wear leveling is not specified in the SD card standard, so no manufacturer is compelled to follow SanDisk's lead.

Note that wear leveling applies to read/write file systems. If the file system is mounted read-only, no erase and program operations are occurring inside the card. So no "erase wear" is taking place. But do take into account all of the mounted partitions on the same media.

If you are using your Raspberry Pi for educational purposes, you can probably ignore the issue. However, using known brands like SanDisk can provide you with additional quality assurance. Consider also the advantage of documented overprovisioning and wear leveling characteristics.

■ **Caution** Some brands of SD cards have been reported not to work with the Raspberry Pi, so the brand/product issue cannot be totally ignored.

CHAPTER 9

■ ■ ■

UART

The Raspberry Pi has a UART interface to allow it to perform serial data communications. The data lines used are 3.3 V logic-level signals and should *not* be connected to TTL logic (+5 V) (they also are *not RS-232 compatible)*. To communicate with equipment using RS-232, you will need a converter module.

RS-232 Converter

While an industrious person could build their own RS-232 converter, there is little need to do so when cheap converters are available.

Figure 9-1 shows a MAX232CSE chip interface that I use. (This unit supports only the RX and TX lines.) When searching for a unit, be sure that you get one that works with 3 V logic levels. Some units work only with TTL (+5 V) logic, which would be harmful to the Pi. The MAX232CSE chip will support 3 V operation when its VCC supply pin is connected to +3 V.

Figure 9-1. *MAX232CSE interface*

■ **Note**   Throughout this text, we'll refer to *3 V*, knowing that it is precisely 3.3 V.

Figure 9-2 is a schematic excerpt of the UART section of the Raspberry Pi. The UART connections are shown as TXD0 and RXD0.

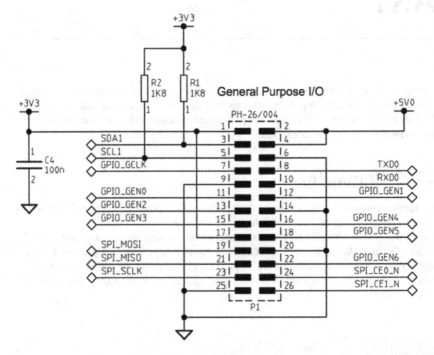

Figure 9-2. *UART interface*

Also when selecting a converter, consider whether you need only the data lines, or the data lines *and the hardware flow control signals*. Some units support only the RX and TX lines. For hardware flow control, you'll also want the CTS and DTR signals. A full RS-232 converter would also include DTR, DSR, and CD signals.

DTE or DCE

When choosing your RS-232 converter, keep in mind that there are two types of serial connections:

> *DCE*: Data communications equipment (female connector)

> *DTE*: Data terminal equipment (male connector)

A normal USB serial adapter (for a laptop, for example) will present a DTE (male) connector. The wiring of this cable is such that it expects to plug into to a DCE (female) connection. When this holds true for your Raspberry Pi's adapter, the laptop's serial adapter can plug straight into the DCE (female) connector, *eliminating* the need for a crossover cable or null modem.

Consequently, for your Pi, choose a RS-232 converter that provides a female (DCE) connector. Likewise, make sure that you acquire for the laptop/desktop a cable or USB device that presents a male (DTE) connection. Connecting DTE to DTE or DCE to DCE requires a crossover cable, and depending on the cable, a "gender mender" as well. It is best to get things "straight" right from the start.

Assuming that you used a DCE converter for the Pi, connect the RS-232 converter's 3 V logic TX to the Pi's TXD0 and the RX to the Pi's RXD0 data lines.

All this business about DCE and DTR has always been rather confusing. If you also find this confusing, there is another practical way to look at it. Start with the connectors and the cable(s) that you plan to use. Make sure they mate at both ends and that the serial cable is known to be a *straight cable* (instead of a *crossover*). Once those physical problems are taken care of, you can get the wiring correct. Connect the TX to RX, and RX to TX. In other words, *you* wire the crossover in your own wiring between the RS-232 adapter and the Raspberry Pi. The important thing to remember is that somewhere the transmitting side needs to send a signal into the RX (receiving) side, in both directions.

■ **Note** A straight serial cable will connect pin 2 to pin 2, and pin 3 to pin 3 on a DB9 or DB25 cable. A crossover cable will cross these two, among other signal wire changes.

RS-232

RS-232 is the traditional name for a series of standards related to serial communication. It was first introduced by the Radio Sector of the EIA in 1962.[46] The first data terminals were teletypewriters (DTE) communicating with modems (DCE). Early serial communications were plagued by incompatibilities until later standards evolved.

A serial link includes two data lines, with data being transmitted from a terminal and received by the same terminal. In addition to these data lines are several handshaking signals (such as RTS and CTS). By default, these are not provided for by the Raspberry Pi.

Figure 9-3 shows a serial signal transmission, with time progressing from left to right. RS-232 equipment expects a signal that varies between –15 V and +15 V.

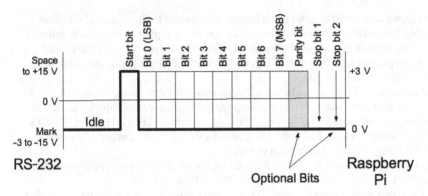

Figure 9-3. *Serial signal*

The standard states that the signal is considered to be in a *mark state*, when the voltage is between –3 and –15 V. The signal is considered in a *space state* if the voltage is between +3 and +15 V. The RS-232 data line is in the mark state when the line is idle.

Start Bit

When an asynchronous character of data is to be sent, the line first shifts to a space level for the duration of 1 bit. This is known as the *start bit* (0). Data bits immediately follow.

Asynchronous lines do not use a clock signal like synchronous links. The asynchronous receiver must have a clock matching the same baud rate as the transmitter. The receiver samples the line 16 times in the bit cell time to determine its value. Sampling helps to avoid a noise pulse from triggering a false data read.

Data Bits

Data bits immediately follow the start bit, least significant bit first. A space is a 0 data bit, while mark represents a 1 bit. Early teletype equipment used 5 data bits sending characters in the 5-bit Baudot code.[47] For this reason, serial ports can be configured for 5, 6, 7, or 8 data bits. Before the ASCII character set was extended to 8 bits, it was common to use 7-bit serial data.

Parity Bit

An optional parity bit can be generated when transmitting or can be detected on the receiving side. The parity can be odd, even, or stick (mark or space). The most commonly used setting today is No Parity, which saves 1-bit time for faster communication. Older equipment often used parity to guard against errors from noisy serial lines. Odd parity is preferred over even because it forces at least one signal transition in the byte's transmission. This helps with the data reliability.

Mark or space parity is unusual and has limited usefulness. Mark parity could be used along with 2 stop bits to effectively provide 3 stop bits for very slow teletypewriter equipment. Mark or space parity reduces the effective throughput of data without providing any benefit, except possibly for diagnostic purposes. Table 9-1 summarizes the various parity configurations.

Table 9-1. *RS-232 Parity Settings*

Parity	X	Notes
None	N	No parity bit
Even	E	1 if even number of data 1-bits
Odd	O	1 if odd number of data 1-bits
Mark	M	Always at mark level (1)
Space	S	Always at space level (0)

Stop Bit(s)

Asynchronous communication requires synchronizing the receiver with the transmitter. For this reason, 1 or more stop bits exist so that the receiver can synchronize with the leading edge of the next start bit. In effect, each stop bit followed by a start bit provides built-in synchronization.

Many UARTs support 1, 1.5, or 2 stop bits. The Broadcom SoC supports 1 or 2 stop bits only. The use of 2 stop bits was common for teletypewriter equipment and probably rarely used today. Using 1 stop bit increases the overall data throughput. Table 9-2 summarizes the stop-bit configurations.

Table 9-2. *Stop-Bit Configuration*

Stop Bits	Description
1	1 stop bit
1.5	1.5 stop bits (†)
2	2 stop bits

†Unsupported by the Raspberry Pi

Baud Rate

The *baud rate* is calculated from bits per second, which includes the start, data, parity, and stop bits. A link using 115200 baud, with no parity and 1 stop bit, provides the following data byte rate:

$$D_{rate} = \frac{B}{s + d + p + S}$$

$$= \frac{115200}{1 + 8 + 0 + 1}$$

$$= 11,520 \text{ bytes/sec}$$

where

> B is the baud rate.
>
> s is the start bit (always 1).
>
> d is the number of data bits (5, 6, 7, or 8).
>
> p is the parity bit (0 or 1).
>
> S is the stop bit (1, 1.5, or 2).

The 115200 baud link allows 11,250 bytes per second. If a parity bit is added, the throughput is reduced:

$$D_{rate} = \frac{115200}{1 + 8 + 1 + 1}$$

$$= 10,472.7 \text{ bytes/sec}$$

The addition of a parity bit reduces the transmission rate to 10,472.7 bytes per second.

Table 9-3 lists the standard baud rates that a serial link can be configured for on the Raspberry Pi.

Table 9-3. *Standard Baud Rates*

Rate	Notes
75	Teletypewriters
110	Teletypewriters
300	Low-speed (acoustic) modem
1200	
2400	
4800	
9600	
19200	
38400	
57600	
115200	Raspberry Pi console

Break

With asynchronous communication, it is also possible to send and receive a *break signal*. This is done by stretching the start bit beyond the data bits and the stop bit(s), and eventually returning the line to the mark state. When the receiver sees a space instead of a mark for the stop bit, it sees a *framing error*.

Some UARTs distinguish between a framing error and a break by noting how long the line remains in the space state. A simple framing error can happen as part of noisy serial line communications (particularly when modems were used) and normally attributed to a received character error. Without break detection, it is possible to assume that a break has been received when several framing errors occur in a sequence. Short sequences of framing errors, however, can also just indicate a mismatch in baud rates between the two end points.

Flow Control

Any link that transmits from one side to a receiver on the other side has the problem of flow control. Imagine a factory assembly line where parts to be assembled arrive at the worker's station faster than he can assemble them. At some point, the conveyor belt must be temporarily stopped, or some parts will not get assembled. Alternatively, if the conveyor belt is reduced in speed, the assembly worker will always be able to keep up, but perhaps at a slower than optimal pace.

Unless the serial link receiver can process every character of data as fast as it arrives, it will need flow control. The simplest approach is to simply reduce the baud rate, so that the receiver can always keep up. But this isn't always satisfactory and leads to a reduced overall throughput. A logging application might be able to write the information quickly, except when writes occur to an SD card, for example.

A better approach is to signal to the transmitter to stop sending when the receiver is bogged down. Once the receiver catches up, it can then tell the transmitter to resume transmission. Note that this problem exists for both sides of a serial link:

- Data transmitted to the terminal (DTE)

- Data transmitted to the data communications equipment (DCE)

Two forms of flow control are used:

- Hardware flow control

- Software flow control

Hardware Flow Control

Hardware flow control uses additional signal lines to regulate the flow of data. The RS-232 standards have quite an elaborate set of signals defined, but the main signals needed for flow control are shown in Table 9-4. Unlike the data line, these signals are inactive in the space state and active in the mark state.

Table 9-4. *Hardware Flow Controls*

DTE	Direction	DCE	Description	Active
RTS	→	RTS	Request to send(†)	Low
CTS	←	CTS	Clear to send(†)	
DSR	←	DSR	Data set ready	Low
DTR	→	DTR	Data terminal ready	

† Primary flow control signals

The most important signals are the ones marked with a dagger in Table 9-4. When CTS is active (mark), for example, the DCE (Pi) is indicating that it is OK to send data. If the DCE gets overwhelmed by the volume of data, the CTS signal will change to the inactive (space) state. Upon seeing this, the DTE (laptop) is required to stop sending data. (Otherwise, loss of data may occur.)

Similarly, the laptop operating as the DTE is receiving data from the DCE (Pi). If the laptop gets overwhelmed with the volume of incoming data, the RTS signal is changed to the inactive state (space). The remote end (DCE) is then expected to cease transmitting. When the laptop has caught up, it will reassert RTS, giving the DCE permission to resume.

The DTR and DSR signals are intended to convey the readiness of the equipment at each end. If the terminal was deemed not ready (DTR), DSR is not made active by the DCE. Similarly, the terminal will not assert DTR unless it is ready. In modern serial links, DTR and DSR are often assumed to be true, leaving only CTS and RTS to handle flow control.

Where flow control is required, hardware flow control is considered more reliable than software flow control.

Software Flow Control

To simplify the cabling and the supporting hardware for serial communications, the hardware flow controls can be omitted/ignored. In its place, a data protocol is used instead.

Initially, each end of the link assumes readiness for reception of data. Data is sent until an XOFF character is received, indicating that transmission should stop. The receiver sends the XON character when it is ready to resume reception again. These software flow control characters are shown in Table 9-5.

Table 9-5. *Software Flow Control Characters*

Code	Meaning	ASCII	Hex	Keyboard
XOFF	Pause transmission	DC3	13	Control-S
XON	Resume transmission	DC1	11	Control-Q

In a terminal session, the keyboard commands can be used to control the serial connection. For example, if information is displaying too fast, the user can type Ctrl-S to cause the transmission to stop. Pressing Ctrl-Q allows it to resume.

The disadvantages of software flow control include the following:

1. Line noise can prevent the receiver from seeing the XOFF character and can lead to loss of data (causing data overrun).

2. Line noise can prevent the remote end from seeing the XON character and can fail to resume transmission (causing a link "lockup").

3. Line noise can cause a false XON/XOFF character to be received (data loss or link lockup).

4. The delay in the remote end seeing a transmitted XOFF character can cause loss of data if the receiving buffer is full.

5. The XON and XOFF characters cannot be used for data in the transmission.

Problems 1 to 3 can cause link lockups or data loss to occur. Problem 4 is avoidable if the buffer notifies the other end early enough to prevent a buffer overflow. Problem 5 is an issue for binary data transmission.

Raspberry Pi UARTs

The Raspberry Pi supports two UARTs:

UART	Driver	Node	GPIO	ALT
UART0	drivers/tty/serial/amba- pl011.c	/dev/ttyAMA0	14 & 15	0
UART1	The mini has no driver.		14 & 15	5

Some websites have incorrectly stated that the mini UART is the one being used. But this does not jibe with the Broadcom documentation, nor the Raspbian Linux device driver. The Broadcom *BCM2835 ARM Peripherals* manual states that the mini UART is UART1. UART1 is available only as alternate function 5 for GPIO 14 and 15. Raspbian Linux boots up using alternate function 0 for GPIO 14 and 15, providing the UART0 peripheral instead. Finally, the source code for the device driver references PL011 in the naming throughout.

ARM PL011 UART

By default, UART0 is provided after reset and boot-up, on GPIO 14 (TX) and 15 (RX), configured as alternate function 0 (Table 9-6). UART0 is the full UART, referred to as the ARM PL011 UART. Broadcom refers the interested reader to the *ARM PrimeCell UART (PL011) Revision r1p5 Technical Reference Manual* for more information.

Table 9-6. *UART0 Pins*

Function	GPIO	P1/P5	ALT	Direction	Description
TXD	14	P1-08	0	Out	DTE transmitted data
RXD	15	P1-10	0	In	DTE received data
RTS	17	P1-11	3	Out	Request to send
CTS	30	P5-05	3	In	Clear to send

RTS/CTS Access

Hardware flow controls CTS and RTS are available on GPIO 30 and 17, respectively, when configured. By default these are GPIO inputs, but this can be changed. To gain access to the UART's CTS and RTS signals, configure GPIO 30 and 17 to *alternate function 3*. Table 9-6 summarizes the connections that are used by the UART.

The following short C program shows how to gain access to these signals. The listing for the included source file gpio_io.c is given in the "Direct Register Access" section of Chapter 10.

```
1   /****************************************************************
2    * rtscts.c     Configure GPIO 17 & 30 for RTS & CTS
3    ****************************************************************/
4
5   #include <stdio.h>
6   #include <stdlib.h>
7   #include <fcntl.h>
8   #include <unistd.h>
9   #include <errno.h>
10  #include <setjmp.h>
11  #include <sys/mman.h>
12  #include <signal.h>
13
14  #include "gpio_io.c"    /* GPIO routines */
15
16  static inline void
17  gpio_setalt(intgpio, unsigned alt) {
18          INP_GPIO(gpio);
19          SET_GPIO_ALT(gpio, alt);
20  }
21
22  int
```

```
23  main(int argc, char **argv) {
24
25          gpio_init();           /* Initialize GPIO access */
26          gpio_setalt(17, 3);    /* GPIO 17 ALT = 3 */
27          gpio_setalt(30, 3);    /* GPIO 3 0 ALT = 3 */
28          return 0;
29  }
30
31  /* End rtscts.c */
```

PL011 UART Features

The Broadcom *BCM2835 ARM Peripherals* manual states that the following features are *unsupported*:

- *No* Infrared Data Association (IrDA) support

- *No* Serial InfraRed (SIR) protocol encoder/decoder (endec)

- *No* direct memory access (DMA)

- *No* support for signals DCD, DSR, DTR, and RI

The following features *are* supported, however:

- Separate 16×8 transmit and 16×12 receive FIFO buffers

- Programmable baud rate generator

- False start-bit detection

- Line-break generation and detection

- Support of control functions CTS and RTS

- Programmable hardware flow control

- Fully programmable serial interface characteristics:

  - Data can be 5, 6, 7, or 8 bits.

  - Even, odd, mark, space, or no-parity bit generation and detection.

  - 1 or 2 stop-bit generation.

  - Baud rate generation, DC up to UARTCLK/16.

Broadcom also states that there are some differences between its implementation of the UART and the 16C650 UART. But these are mostly device driver details:

- Receive FIFO trigger levels are 1/8, 1/4, 1/2, 3/4, and 7/8.

- Transmit FIFO trigger levels are 1/8, 1/4, 1/2, 3/4, and 7/8.

- The internal register map address space and the bit function of each register differ.

- 1.5 stop bits is *not* supported.

- *No* independent receive clock.

The only real concern to the application developer is that the 1.5 stop-bits configuration option is not available, which is rarely used these days anyway.

If you need the RS-232 DCD, DSR, DTR, and RI signals, these can be implemented using GPIO input and output pins (along with the appropriate RS-232 line-level shifters). These are relatively slow-changing signals, which can easily be handled in user space. The one limitation of this approach, however, is that the hang-up TTY controls provided by the device driver will be absent. To change that, the device driver source code could be modified to support these signals using GPIO. The Raspbian Linux module of interest for this is as follows:

```
drivers/tty/serial/amba-pl011.c
```

Exclusive Serial Line Use

As outlined in the "Available Consoles" section in Chapter 5 of *Raspberry Pi System Software Reference* (Apress, 2014), the serial device /dev/ttyAMA0 is easily applied as a serial console device. However, some Raspberry Pi application developers will want to use that serial interface for application purposes, instead of a console. Without taking measures for exclusive access, the console will write to your serial peripheral and respond to its input as well (as root console commands).

Even if you turned off the console, there can still be unwanted interaction from a login prompt.

Procedure

Use the following steps to configure exclusive serial port access:

1. Eliminate console references to console=ttyAMA0,... in the files:

   a. /boot/cmline.txt

   b. /boot/config.txt (check option cmdline="...")

2. Eliminate the kernel debugging option kgdboc=ttyAMA0,...
    as outlined for the console in step 1.

3. Eliminate the login prompt caused by the /etc/inittab entry.
    Look for ttyAMA0 and comment the line out. The line will look
    something like T0:23:respawn:/sbin/getty -L ttyAMA0
    115200 vt100.

With these steps accomplished, reboot. The device /dev/ttyAMA0 should be
available exclusively for your application to use.

Verification

To check that /etc/inittab has not launched a getty process, use the following after
rebooting:

```
$ ps aux | grep ttyAMA0
```

No entries should appear.
To check that you have eliminated all kernel console references to the device, you
can use the following:

```
$ grep ttyAMA0 /proc/cmdline
```

Serial API

The Linux operating system provides access to serial port functions through a family of
system and library calls. Most of these require that you have an open file descriptor for
the serial device driver being used. For the Raspberry Pi, this will usually be the device
/dev/ttyAMA0. Full information can be had from these man pages:

- tcgetattr(3)
- tty_ioctl(4)-ioctl(2) equivalents to tcgetattr(3)

The bulk of the developer work for serial ports is configuration of the serial driver:

- Physical characteristics: baud rate, data bits, parity, and stop bits
- Driver processing characteristics: raw or cooked mode, for
  example

Once the driver is configured, the software developer is able to use the usual
read(2)/readv(2), write(2)/writev(2), select(2), or poll(2) system calls.
For an example program using some of this API, see the "Software" section in
Chapter 6 of *Experimenting with Raspberry Pi* (Apress, 2014).

Header Files

Programs involved in altering TTY settings will want to include the following include files:

```
#include <termios.h>
#include <unistd.h>
```

open(2)

Most of the serial operations in this section require an open file descriptor to the TTY device being used. For the Raspberry Pi UART, you'll want to specify /dev/ttyAMA0.

```
int fd;

fd = open("/dev/ttyAMA0",O_RDWR); /* Open for reading and writing */
if ( fd < 0 ) {
    perror("Opening/dev/ttyAMA0");
```

You may need to take special measures to gain access to the device, since by default it will be protected. Note the permissions and user/group ownership:

```
$ ls -l /dev/ttyAMA0
crw-rw---1 root tty 204, 64 Feb 9 13:12  /dev/ttyAMA0
```

struct termios

Many of the serial port configuration options require the use of the structure termios:

```
struct termios {
    tcflag_t  c_iflag;     /* input mode flags */
    tcflag_t  c_oflag;     /* output mode flags */
    tcflag_t  c_cflag;     /* control mode flags */
    tcflag_t  c_lflag;     /* local mode flags */
    cc_t      c_line;      /* line discipline */
    cc_t      c_cc[NCCS];  /* control characters */
    speed_t   c_ispeed;    /* input speed */
    speed_t   c_ospeed;    /* output speed */
};
```

The tables in the following sections describe the C language macros used for the members of the termios structure:

- Table 9-7 lists the macros for member c_iflag.

Table 9-7. *Input (c_iflag) Flags*

Flag	Set	Description	Flag	Description
BRKINT	T	Break causes SIGINT else 0x00	ISTRIP	Strip off eighth bit
	F	Break reads as 0x00	INLCR	Translate NL to CR
IXANY		Any character will resume	IUTF8	Input is UTF8 charset
IXOFF		Enable input XON/XOFF	ICRNL	Translate CR to NL
IXON		Enable output XON/XOFF	IGNBRK	Ignore break
IGNPAR		Ignore framing and parity errors	IGNCR	Ignore CR
IUCLC		Translate uppercase to lowercase		
INPCK		Enable parity checking		
PARMRK	T	Prefix framing/parity error with \377		
	F	Don't prefix with \377 (byte reads 0)		

- Table 9-8 lists the macros for member c_oflag.

Table 9-8. *Output (c_oflag) Flags*

Flag	Description	Flag	Description
CR0	CR delay mask 0	OFDEL	Fill character is DEL else NUL
CR1	CR delay mask 1	OFILL	Use fill characters instead of timed delay
CR2	CR delay mask 2	OLCUC	Translate lowercase to uppercase
CR3	CR delay mask 3	ONLCR	Translate NL to CR-NL
CRDLY	CR delay: apply CR0-CR3	ONLRET	Don't output CR
FF0	FF delay mask 0	ONOCR	Don't output CR at column 0
FF1	FF delay mask 1	OPOST	Enable output processing
FFDLY	FF delay: apply FF0-FF1	TAB0	Tab delay mask 0
NL0	NL delay mask 0	TAB1	Tab delay mask 1
NL1	NL delay mask 1	TAB2	Tab delay mask 1
NLDLY	NL delay: apply NL0-NL1	TAB3	Tab delay mask 2
OCRNL	Translate CR to NL	TABDLY	Tab delay: apply TAB0-TAB3

•   Table 9-9 lists the macros for member c_cflag.

Table 9-9. *Control (c_cflag) Flags*

Flag	Baud	Flag	Baud	Flag	Description
B0	Hang-up	B115200	115,200	CLOCAL	Ignore modem controls
B50	50	B230400	230,400	CMSPAR	Stick parity
B75	75	B460800	460,800	CREAD	Enable receiver
B110	110	B500000	500,000	CRTSCTS	Enable RTS/CTS flow
B134	134	B576000	576,000	CS5	5 data bits
B150	150	B921600	921,600	CS6	6 data bits
B200	200	B1000000	1,000,000	CS7	7 data bits
B300	300	B1152000	1,152,000	CS8	8 data bits
B600	600	B1500000	1,500,000	CSIZE	Data bits mask
B1200	1,200	B2000000	2,000,000	CSTOPB	2 stop bits (else 1)
B1800	1,800	B2500000	2,500,000	HUPCL	Modem control hang-up
B2400	2,400	B3000000	3,000,000	PARENB	Enable parity
B4800	4,800	B3500000	3,500,000	PARODD	Odd or stick = 1 parity
B9600	9,600	B4000000	4,000,000	CBAUD	Rate mask
B19200	19,200			CBAUDEX	Extended mask
B38400	38,400			CIBAUD	Input rate mask
B57600	57,600			EXTA	External A
				EXTB	External B

- Table 9-10 lists the macros for member c_lflag.

Table 9-10. *Local (c_lflag) Flags*

Flag	Description	Flag	Description
ECHOCTL	Echo controls as ^X	ECHO	Echo input
IEXTEN	Enable input processing	ECHOE	Erase previous char
PENDIN	Reprint upon reading	ECHOK	Erase line on kill
ECHOKE	Erase each char on kill	ISIG	Generate signals
ECHONL	Echo NL even if !ECHO	NOFLSH	No flush on signal
ECHOPRT	Print chars during erase	TOSTOP	Send SIGTTOU
ICANON	Enable canonical mode	XCASE	Terminal is uppercase

- Table 9-11 lists the macros for member c_cc.

Table 9-11. *Special (c_cc) Characters*

Macro	Description	Macro	Description
VEOF	End-file (^D)	VQUIT	Quit (^\)
VEOL	End line (NUL)	VREPRINT	Reprint (^R)
VEOL2	End line 2	VSTART	· XON (^Q)
VERASE	Erase (^H)	VSTOP	XOFF (^S)
VINTR	Interrupt (^C)	VSUSP	Suspend (^Z)
VKILL	Kill (^U)	VTIME	Time-out decsecs
VLNEXT	Literal next (^V)	VWERASE	Word erase (^W)
VMIN	Min chars to read		

tcgetattr(3)

Before you make changes to the serial port settings, you will want to retrieve the current settings in case you later need to restore them. This also greatly simplifies configuration, allowing you to change only the settings that need changing.

Use the tcgetattr(3) function to fetch the current serial device settings:

```
int tcgetattr(int fd, struct termios *termios_p);
```

where
  fd is the open TTY file descriptor.
  termios_p is the struct to be filled with current setting information.

```
struct termios term;
int rc;

rc = tcgetattr(fd,&term);
if ( rc < 0 ) {
    perror("tcgetattr(3)");
```

tcsetattr(3)

When the termios structure has been defined with the serial parameters you wish to use, the tcsetattr(3) call is used to set them in the device driver:

```
int tcsetattr(
  int fd,
  int optional_actions,
  const struct termios *termios_p
);
```

where
  fd is the open TTY file descriptor to change.
  optional_actions is one of three actions (listed in the following table).
  termios_p is a pointer to the new settings to be applied.
  The three choices for optional_actions are as follows:

optional_actions	Meaning
TCSANOW	The change occurs immediately.
TCSADRAIN	Change occurs after all output has been sent.
TCSAFLUSH	As TCSADRAIN, but pending input is discarded.

The following shows an example of use:

```
struct termios term;
int rc;

...
rc = tcsetattr(fd,TCSADRAIN,&term);
if ( rc < 0 ) {
    perror("tcsetattr(3)");
```

tcsendbreak(3)

A break signal can be transmitted to the remote end by calling the tcsendbreak(3) function:

```
int tcsendbreak(int fd, int duration);
```

where
  fd is the open TTY file descriptor.
  duration is the amount of time to use to represent a break.

When the argument duration is zero, it sends a break signal lasting between 0.25 and 0.5 seconds. When the argument is nonzero, the man page states that some implementation-defined amount of time is used instead.

```
int rc;

rc = tcsendbreak(fd,0);
if ( rc < 0 ) {
    perror("tcsendbreak(3)");
```

tcdrain(3)

The function tcdrain(3) can be used to block the execution of the calling program until all of the output characters have been transmitted out of the UART:

```
int tcdrain(int fd);
```

where
  fd is the open TTY file descriptor. An example follows:

```
int rc;

rc = tcdrain(fd);
if ( rc < 0 ) {
    perror("tcdrain(3)");
```

tcflush(3)

The tcflush(3) call can be used to flush pending input or output data from the serial port buffers.

```
int tcflush(int fd, int queue_selector);
```

where
fd is the open TTY file descriptor.
queue_selector determines which queue(s) are to be flushed.
The following values are used for the queue_selector argument:

queue_selector	Description
TCIFLUSH	Flushes unread incoming data
TCOFLUSH	Flushes untransmitted output data
TCIOFLUSH	Flushes both unread and untransmitted data

The following example flushes pending input data:

```
int rc;

rc = tcflush(fd,TCIFLUSH);
```

tcflow(3)

Various flow control operations can be performed by calling the tcflow(3) function:

```
int tcflow(int fd, int action);
```

where
fd is the open TTY file descriptor.
action is the flow control action required (as shown in the following table).
The valid choices for action are as follows:

action	Description
TCOOFF	Suspends output (transmission stops)
TCOON	Resumes output
TCIOFF	Immediately sends a STOP character to stop the remote device
TCION	Transmits a START character to resume the remote device

The following example shows the program immediately suspending output:

```
int rc;

rc = tcflow(fd,TCOOFF);
if ( rc < 0 ) {
    perror("tcflow (3)");
```

cfmakeraw(3)

The cfmakeraw(3) function is a *convenience routine* to establish raw mode, where no special data conversions or mappings occur. The caller should first call upon tcgetattr(3) to define the initial termios structure settings. Then cfmakeraw(3) can be used to adjust those settings for raw mode:

```
void cfmakeraw(struct termios *termios_p);
```

where
    termios_p is a pointer to a struct populated with the serial device's current settings, to be altered.

Note that *no file descriptor is provided* since this function doesn't actually change anything beyond the data structure that was passed to it. After calling cfmakeraw(3), the user will need to use cfsetattr(3) to inform the driver of the changes.

```
struct termios term;
int rc;

rc = cfgetattr(fd,&term);  /* Get settings */
cfmakeraw(&term);          /* Alter settings for raw mode */
rc = tcsetattr(fd,TCSADRAIN,&term); /* Apply the settings */
```

Calling cfmakeraw(3) is equivalent to manually applying the following changes:

```
struct termios term;
...
term.c_iflag &= ~(IGNBRK | BRKINT | PARMRK | ISTRIP
                | INLCR | IGNCR  | ICRNL  | IXON);
term.c_oflag &= ~OPOST;
term.c_lflag &= ~(ECHO  | ECHONL | ICANON | ISIG | IEXTEN);
term.c_cflag &= ~(CSIZE | PARENB);
term.c_cflag |=CS8;
```

This is a good place to pause and discuss what raw mode is. There are two forms of serial I/O supported by Linux (and Unix generally):
    Cooked mode: The input, output, and echoing functions are modified/performed by the kernel.
    Raw mode: The input/output data is sent to/from the application unchanged by the kernel.

The serial port developer, wishing to communicate with a serial device or AVR class microcontroller, will be very interested in raw mode. Using raw mode, the data you transmit is sent unmodified to its destination. Likewise, the data received is received as it was originally transmitted. Cooked mode, which is the norm, is a very different beast.

The original purpose of serial lines for Unix was the handling of user interaction using terminal I/O (this is still true for the serial port console). Many terminal processing functions were considered common enough among applications to centralize them in the kernel. This saved the application from having to deal with these physical aspects and lead to consistency in their handling. This terminal handling is affectionately known as *cooked mode*.

The main areas of cooked mode processing are as follows:

> *Input processing*: The type of kernel processing performed on serial input data (like backspace processing)

> *Output processing*: The type of kernel processing performed on serial output data (like converting a sent line feed into a carriage return and line-feed pair)

> *Local processing*: Involving input *and* output, processing features such as echo

> *Control processing*: Other serial controls

We can get a sense of how raw mode differs from cooked mode by looking at what cfmakeraw(3) changes. Looking at

```
term.c_iflag &= ~ (IGNBRK | BRKINT | PARMRK | ISTRIP
                 | INLCR | IGNCR | ICRNL | IXON);
```

we see that the following input processing features are disabled:

Flag	Description	Setting
IGNBRK	Ignore break	Disabled
BRKINT	Break reads as 0x00	Disabled
PARMRK	Don't prefix with \377 (byte reads 0)	Disabled
ISTRIP	Strip off eighth bit	Disabled
INLCR	Translate NL to CR	Disabled
IGNCR	Ignore CR	Disabled
ICRNL	Translate CR to NL	Disabled
IXON	Enable output XON/XOFF	Disabled

Disabling ISTRIP prevents the kernel from stripping the high-order bit in the byte. Disabling INLCR, ICRNL prevents the substitution of NL or CR characters (for input). Disabling IGNCR prevents the kernel from deleting the CR character from the input stream. Disabling IXON disables software flow control so that the characters XON and XOFF can be read by the application program.

Looking at the output processing changes,

```
term.c_oflag &= ~OPOST;
```

we see that the following change applies:

Flag	Description	Setting
OPOST	Enable output processing	Disabled

This disables all output processing features with one flag.

Local processing includes both input and output. The following local processing flags are changed:

```
term.c_lflag &= ~(ECHO | ECHONL | ICANON | ISIG| IEXTEN);
```

From this, we see that these local processing features are disabled:

Flag	Description	Setting
ECHO	Echo input	Disabled
ECHONL	Echo NL even if !ECHO	Disabled
ICANON	Enable canonical mode	Disabled
ISIG	Generate signals	Disabled
IEXTEN	Enable input processing	Disabled

Disabling ICANON means that all special nonsignal characters defined in c_cc are disregarded (like VERASE). Disabling ISIG means that there will be no signals sent to your application for characters like VINTR. Disabling IEXTEN disables other c_cc character processing like VEOL2, VLNEXT, VREPRINT, VWERASE, and the IUCLC flag. Disabling ECHO and ECHONL disables two aspects of character echoing.

Finally, the following control aspects are changed:

```
term.c_cflag &= ~ (CSIZE | PARENB);
term.c_cflag |= CS8;
```

111

meaning that:

Flag	Description	Setting
CSIZE	Data bits mask	Masked-out data bits
PARENB	Generate/detect parity	Disabled
CS8	8 data bits	Set to 8-bit data

The CSIZE masking is used to reset the data bits field to zeros. This allows the CS8 bit pattern to be or-ed in later, setting the data bits value to 8 bits. Disabling the PARENB flag causes parity generation on output to be disabled, and disables parity checking on input. If your raw link requires parity generation and checking, you'll need to undo this particular change in your own code.

You can see from this list that a plethora of special processing is altered to go from cooked mode to raw mode. It is no wonder that this support routine was made available.

cfgetispeed(3)

The current *input* baud rate for the line can be queried by the cfgetispeed(3) function:

```
speed_t cfgetispeed(const struct termios *termios_p);
```

where
    termios_p is the pointer to the structure containing the terminal configuration.

Because the termios structure has been extended and modified over the years, this function provides a more portable way to extract the input baud rate, including the more recently added higher baud rates.

```
struct termios term;
speed_t baud_rate;
baud_rate = cfgetispeed(&term);
```

cfgetospeed(3)

The current *output* baud rate can be extracted from the termios structure with

```
speed_t cfgetospeed(const struct termios *termios_p);
```

where
    termios_p is the pointer to the structure containing the terminal configuration.

Because the termios structure has been extended and modified over the years, this function provides a portable way to extract the output baud rate, including the more recently added higher baud rates.

cfsetispeed(3)

The cfsetispeed(3) function permits a portable way to establish an input baud rate in the termios structure:

```
int cfsetispeed(struct termios *termios_p, speed_t speed);
```

where

termios_p is the pointer to the TTY configuration structure to be modified.

speed is the input baud rate to apply.

Note that this function only updates the termios data structure and has no direct effect on the device being used.

```
struct termios term;
int rc;

rc = cfsetispeed(&term,115200);
if ( rc < 0 ) {
    perror("cfsetispeed(3)");
```

cfsetospeed(3)

The cfsetospeed(3) function sets the output baud rate in the termios structure:

```
int cfsetospeed(struct termios *termios_p, speed_t speed);
```

where

termios_p is the pointer to the TTY configuration structure being modified.

speed is the output baud rate to apply.

Note that this function only updates the termios data structure with no direct effect on the device being used.

```
struct termios term;
int rc;

rc = cfsetospeed(&term,9600);
if ( rc < 0 ) {
    perror("cfsetospeed(3)");
```

cfsetspeed(3)

Most serial communication uses a common baud rate for transmitting and receiving. For this reason, this is the preferred function to invoke for establishing both the input and output baud rates:

```
int cfsetspeed(struct termios *termios_p, speed_t speed);
```

where

termios_p is the pointer to the TTY configuration structure to be modified.

speed is the input and output baud rate to apply.

Note that this function only updates the termios data structure with no direct effect on the device being used.

```
struct termios term;
int rc;

rc = cfsetspeed(&term,9600);
if ( rc < 0 ) {
    perror("cfsetsspeed(3)");
```

read(2)

The read(2) system call can be used for reading from the serial port, in addition to normal Linux files and other devices:

```
#include <unistd.h>

ssize_t read(int fd, void *buf, size_t count);
```

where

fd is the open file descriptor to read from.

buf is the buffer to read the data into.

count is the maximum number of bytes to read.

returns an int, where

-1 indicates an error, with the error code found in errno.

0 indicates that the serial port has been closed with the end-of-file character.

>0 indicates the number of bytes read.

The errors that pertain to blocking calls on a serial port include the following:

Error	Description
EBADF	fd is not a valid file descriptor.
EFAULT	buf is outside your accessible address space.
EINTR	The call was interrupted by a signal before any data was read.

More will be said about EINTR near the end of this chapter.

The following example reads up to 256 bytes into the array buf, from the serial port open on the file unit fd:

```
int fd;          /* Opened serial port */
char buf[256];
int rc;

rc = read(fd,buf,sizeof buf);
if ( rc < 0 ) {
    fprintf(stderr,"%s: reading serial port.\n",strerror(errno));
    ...
} else if ( !rc ) {
    /* End file */
} else {
    /* Process rc bytes in buf[] */
}
```

write(2)

To transmit data on a serial link, you can use the write(2) system call:

```
#include <unistd.h>

ssize_t write(int fd, const void *buf, size_t count);
```

where
    fd is the file unit of the opened serial port.
    buf is the buffer containing the bytes to be transmitted.
    count is the number of bytes to transmit.
returns an int, where

> -1 indicates that an error has occurred, with the error found in errno.
>
> 0 indicates no bytes were transmitted (end-of-file, port was closed).
>
> >0 indicates the number of bytes transmitted.

The possible errors related to blocking calls for serial port writes include the following:

Error	Description
EBADF	fd is not a valid file descriptor or is not open for writing.
EFAULT	buf is outside your accessible address space.
EINTR	The call was interrupted by a signal before any data was written.

Normally, only an error (-1) or a value of count is returned. If the serial port was opened for *nonblocking* I/O, the returned count can be *less* than the requested count (this mode of operation is not discussed here). In blocking mode (which we are assuming here), the call will return only when the full count requested has been written. Any failure would otherwise result in an error being returned instead.

The following is an example of its use, as it pertains to a serial port:

```
int fd;
char buf[256];
int rc, n;

strcpy(buf,"Hello World!\n");
n = strlen(buf);

rc = write(fd,buf,n);
if ( rc < 0 ) {
    fprintf(stderr,"%s: writing serial link.\n",strerror(errno));
    ...
}
assert(rc == n);
```

readv(2) and writev(2)

An often neglected option for reading and writing are the readv(2) and writev(2) system calls. These tend to be more useful for programs that work with packets than for interactive terminal sessions. These are presented because the serial port application developer may want to use a protocol that has more than one buffer containing headers, data, and trailer. Using the scatter-gather routines can enhance your code communicating with an AVR class microcontroller. The use of an I/O vector here is similar in concept to the I/O vectors used by I2C I/O operations in the ioctl(2,I2C_RDWR) system call (see Chapter 12).

```
#include <sys/uio.h>

ssize_t readv(int fd, const struct iovec *iov, int iovcnt);
ssize_t writev(int fd, const struct iovec *iov, int iovcnt);
```

where

fd is the open serial port file descriptor for reading/writing.

iov is the I/O vector directing the reading/writing.

iovcnt is the I/O vector count.

returns an int, where

-1 indicates an error, leaving the error code in errno, see read(2) or write(2).

0 indicates that an end-of-file condition occurred.

>n indicates the actual number of bytes read/written.

The I/O vector is shown here:

```
struct iovec {
    void    *iov_base;    /* Starting address */
    size_t  iov_len;      /* Number of bytes to transfer */
};
```

In the following example, a simple terminal writev(2) system call is used to piece together three pieces of information, to be transmitted to the terminal:

- The text Hello

- The person's name provided in the argument name

- The text !\n\r at the end

One of the advantages of the writev(2) call is its ability to take separate buffers of data and transmit them as a whole in one I/O operation:

```
void
fun(int serport, const char *name) {
    struct iovec iov[3];
    int rc;

    iov[0].iov_base = "Hello";
    iov[0].iov_len = 6;
    iov[1].iov_base = (void *)name;
    iov[1].iov_len = strlen(name);
    iov[2].iov_base = "!\n\r";
    iov[2].iov_len = 3;

    rc = writev(serport,iov,3);
    if ( rc < 0 ) {
        fprintf(stderr,"%s: writev(2)\n",strerror(errno));
        abort();
    }
}
```

Each segment to be transmitted is described by one iov[x] member, each consisting of a buffer pointer and the number of bytes. The writev(2) system call is told how many iov[] entries to use in its third calling argument.

Error EINTR

One error code that afflicts many device I/O system calls is the EINTR error, "Interrupted system call." This error code applies to read(2), readv(2), write(2), and writev(2) on devices that may "block" execution until the required data has been fully read/written. (This also applies to ioctl(2) when I2C I/O is performed.) The EINTR error is not returned for I/O to disk because these I/O calls don't block for a long time (the I/O is to/from a file system disk memory buffer). The application developer should otherwise plan on handling this error.

The EINTR error is the Unix way of working with signals. Consider what happens when your application is waiting for a single keystroke from the user at a terminal (or reading a packet from an AVR class device):

```
rc = read(fd,buf,n);        /* Block until n bytes read */
```

Until that read is satisfied (or the file descriptor is closed), execution will stop there. In the meantime, another process or thread may signal your application to do something, perhaps to shut down and exit. A signal handler like the following is invoked when the signal is handled:

```
static void
sigint_handler(int signo) {
    is_signaled = 1;        /* Please exit this program */
}
```

At this point, your application is in the middle of a system call, waiting to read from the serial port. The system call's registers are saved on the stack frame, and your application has entered into the kernel. The handling of the signal means that the kernel calls your signal handler, placing another stack frame on your current stack.

Because a signal can arrive at any time, there are many things you can't do from within a signal handler. For example, you must not invoke malloc(3) or other non-reentrant functions. Otherwise, you risk doing another malloc(3) inside an interrupted malloc(3), which leads to disaster. The important point here is that a very limited number of safe things can be performed from inside a signal handler.

One thing that *is* safe to do in a signal handler is to set a global variable of some kind, like the is_signaled variable in the example. One problem remains: how does the code blocked in the read(2) call respond to this notification? When the signal handler returns, the application will continue to block trying to read from the serial port.

The Unix solution to this problem is to have the kernel return an error code EINTR after a signal handler receives a signal. In this manner, the read(2) call returns an error, allowing the application program to test whether it received a signal. The following code shows how the simple read(2) call is replaced with a loop that checks whether the signal handler was called:

```
do  {
    rc = read(fd, buf, n);       /* Block until n bytes read */
    if ( is_signaled )
        longjmp(shutdown,1);     /* Shutdown this server */
} while ( rc == -1 && errno == EINTR );

if ( rc == -1 ) {                /* Check for non EINTR errors */
    fprintf(stderr,"%s: read(2)\n",strerror(errno));
    abort();
}
```

In this code snippet, we see that the read(2) call is performed as part of a loop. As long as an error is returned *and the* errno *value is* EINTR, we check for any interesting events (like is_signaled) and repeat the call. If any other type of error occurs or we succeed, we drop out of the loop.

This is the basic template that should be used for any call that might receive EINTR, even if you don't plan to handle signals in your application. Otherwise, you may find that your Pi application may run for weeks and then one day when you least expect it, fail because of a received EINTR error.

CHAPTER 10

GPIO

General-purpose I/O is a topic near to the hearts of Raspberry Pi owners, because this is the interface to the outside world. The BCM2835 is flexibly designed to allow I/O pins to be reconfigured under software control. GPIO 14 can be an input, an output, or operate as a serial port TX data line, for example. This makes the Raspberry Pi very adaptable.

One of the challenges related to the Pi's GPIO interface is that it uses a weak CMOS 3 V interface. The GPIO pins are susceptible to static electricity damage, and the I/O pins are weak drivers (2 to 16 mA). Additionally, GPIO power must be budgeted from the total spare current capacity of 50 mA. Using adapter boards overcomes these problems but adds considerably to the cost. This then provides a fertile area for coming up with cheap and effective roll-your-own solutions.

Pins and Designations

Figures 12-1 and 12-2 show the schematic GPIO connections for the Raspberry Pi. You will notice that the GPIO pins are also designated with the GENx designation. (Gen 7 to 10 was not available prior to version 2.) This may have been an early attempt to follow the Arduino lead of naming their pins digital0 or analog4, for example, in a generic way. It appears, however, that this naming convention has not really caught on among Pi users. Despite this, these names are cross-referenced in Table 10-1. These are probably the preferred first choices when shopping for GPIO pins to use, since they are less likely to be required for special (alternate) functions like UART or SPI.

Table 10-1. *Rev 2.0 GEN and GPIO Designations*

GEN$_x$	GPIO$_y$	Header	GEN$_x$	GPIO$_y$	Header
GEN0	GPIO 17	P1-11	GEN6	GPIO 25	P1-22
GEN1	GPIO 18	P1-12	GEN7	GPIO 28	P5-03
GEN2	GPIO 27	P1-13	GEN8	GPIO 29	P5-04
GEN3	GPIO 22	P1-15	GEN9	GPIO 30	P5-05
GEN4	GPIO 23	P1-16	GEN10	GPIO 31	P5-06
GEN5	GPIO 24	P1-18			

A couple of GPIO pins have pull-up resistors. Figure 10-1 shows that GPIO pins 2 (SDA1) on P1-03, and GPIO 3 (SCL1) on P1-05, have an 1.8 $k\Omega$ pull-up resistor. This should be taken into account if you use these for something other than I2C.

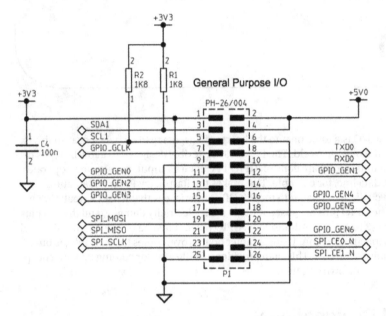

Figure 10-1. *GPIO P1 header*

The layouts of headers P1 and P5, where the GPIO pins are made accessible, are documented in Chapter 3.

■ **Note** P5 was not present prior to version 2, but both Models A and B now include it (without header pins).

Configuration After Reset

Upon reset, most GPIO pins are configured as general-purpose inputs with the exceptions noted in Table 10-2. (Figure 10-2 applies to version 2, Models A and B.) The Pull-up column indicates how the internal pull-up resistor is initially configured. The pull-up resistors apply when the GPIO is configured as an input pin.

Table 10-2. *Rev 2.0 Configuration After Reset*

GPIO	Pull-up	Config	ALT	GPIO	Pull-up	Config	ALT
0	High	Input		17	Low	Input	
1	High	Input		18	Low	Input	
2	High	SDA1	0	21	Low	Input	
3	High	SCL1	0	22	Low	Input	
4	High	Input		23	Low	Input	
5	High	GPCLK1	0	24	Low	Input	
6	High	Output		25	Low	Input	
7	High	Input		27	Low	Output	
8	High	Input		28	-	Input	
9	Low	Input		29	-	Input	
10	Low	Input		30	Low	Input	
11	Low	Input		31	Low	Input	
14	Low	TXD0	0	40	Low	PWM0	0
15	Low	RXD0	0	45	-	PWM1	0
16	Low	Output					

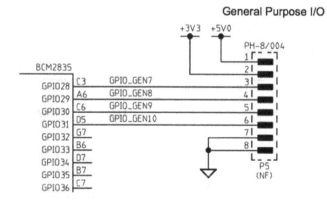

Figure 10-2. *GPIO P5 header*

Pull-up Resistors

As noted earlier, GPIO pins 2 and 3 have an external resistor tied to the +3.3 V rail. The remaining GPIO pins are pulled high or low by an internal 50 $k\Omega$ resistor in the SoC.[56, 48] The internal pull-up resistor is rather weak, and effective at only giving an unconnected GPIO input a defined state. A CMOS input should not be allowed to float midway between its logic, high or low. When pull-up resistance is needed for an external circuit, it is probably best to provide an external pull-up resistor, rather than rely on the weak internal one.

Configuring Pull-up Resistors

The pull-up configuration of a GPIO pin can be configured using the SoC registers GPPUP and GPPUDCLK0/1. (The "Physical Memory" section of Chapter 4 has the physical addresses for these registers.)

The GPPUP register is laid out as follows:

GPPUP Register				
Bits	Field	Description	Type	Reset
31-2	-	Unused	R	0
1-0	PUD	GPIO pin pull-up/down 00 Off—disable pull-up/down	R/W	0
		01 Pull-down enable		
		10 Pull-up enable		
		11 Reserved		

The GPPUDCLK0 register is laid out as follows:

GPPUDCLK0 Register				
Bits	Field	Description	Type	Reset
31-0	PUDCLKn	n = 0..31	R/W	0
		0 No effect		
		1 Assert clock		

Finally, the GPPUDCLK1 register is formatted this way:

GPPUDCLK1 Register				
Bits	Field	Description	Type	Reset
31-22	-	Reserved	R	0
21-0	PUDCLKn	n = 32..53	R/W	0
		0	No effect	
		1	Assert clock	

According to the Broadcom documentation, the general procedure for programming the pull-up resistor is this:

1. Write the pull-up configuration desired in the rightmost 2 bits of the 32-bit GPPUP register. The configuration choices are as follows:

   a. 00: Disable pull-up control.

   b. 01: Enable pull-down control.

   c. 10: Enable pull-up control.

2. Wait 150 cycles to allow the preceding write to be registered.

3. Write a 1-bit to every GPIO position, in the group of 32 GPIO pins being configured. GPIOs 0–31 are configured by register GPPUDCLK0.

4. Wait another 150 cycles to allow step 3 to register.

5. Write 00 to GPPUP to remove the control signal.

6. Wait another 150 cycles to allow step 5 to register.

7. Finally, write to GPPUDCLK0/1 to remove the clock.

The Broadcom procedure may seem confusing because of the word *clock*. Writing to GPPUP and GPPUDCLK0/1 registers by using the preceding procedure is designed to provide a pulse to the internal pull-up resistor flip-flops (their data clock input). First a state is established in step 1, and then the configured 1 bits are clocked high in step 3 (for selected GPIO pins). Step 5 establishes a zero state, which is then sent to the flip-flop clock inputs in step 7.

The documentation also states that the current settings for the pull-up drivers *cannot* be read. This makes sense when you consider that the state is held by these internal flip-flops that were changed by the procedure. (There is no register access available to read these flip-flops.) Fortunately, when configuring the state of a particular GPIO pin, you change only the pins you select by the GPPUDCLK0/1 register. The others remain unchanged.

The program pullup.c, shown next, provides a simple utility to change the pull-up resistor settings. The program listing for gpio_io.c is provided in the "Direct Register Access" section. The source for timed_wait.c is found in the "Source Code" section in Chapter 1 of *Experimenting with Raspberry Pi* (Apress, 2014).

After compiling, the following example changes the GPIO 7 pull-up to high and GPIO 8 to low:

```
$ ./pullup 7=low 8=high
```

```
1   /**********************************************************************
2    * pullup.c : Change the pull-up resistor setting for GPIO pin
3    **********************************************************************/
4
5   #include <stdio.h>
6   #include <stdlib.h>
7   #include <fcntl.h>
8   #include <unistd.h>
9   #include <errno.h>
10  #include <setjmp.h>
11  #include <sys/mman.h>
12  #include <signal.h>
13
14  #include "gpio_io.c"              /* GPIO routines */
15  #include "timed_wait.c"           /* Delay */
16
17  /**********************************************************************
18   * 0x7E200094   GPPUD      GPIO  Pin  Pull-up/down Enable
19   * 0x7E200098   GPPUDCLK0  GPIO  Pin  Pull-up/down Enable Clock 0
20   **********************************************************************/
21
22  #define GPIO_GPPUD              *(ugpio+37)
23  #define GPIO_GPPUDCLK0     *(ugpio+38)
24
25  static inline void
26  gpio_setpullup(int gpio, int pull) {
27          unsigned mask = 1 << gpio;  /* GPIOs 0 to 31 only */
28          unsigned pmask = pull >= 0 ? ( 1 << !! pull) : 0;
29
30          GPIO_GPPUD = pmask;        /* Select pull-up setting */
31          timed_wait (0, 500, 0);
32          GPIO_GPPUDCLK0 = mask;     /* Set the GPIO of interest */
33          timed_wait (0, 500, 0);
34          GPIO_GPPUD = 0;            /* Reset pmask */
35          timed_wait (0, 500, 0);
36          GPIO_GPPUDCLK0 = 0;        /* Set the GPIO of interest */
37          timed_wait (0, 500, 0);
38  }
39
```

```
40   /************************************************************************
41    * Command line arguments are of the form <gpio>={low,high or none},
42    * for example : ./pull-up 7=high 8=low
43    *
44    * Only the first character of the argument after '=' is checked.
45    ************************************************************************/
46   int
47   main(int argc, char **argv) {
48           int x, gpio, p;
49           char arg [64];
50
51           gpio_init();
52
53           for ( x=1; x<argc; ++x ) {
54                   if (sscanf(argv[x],"%d=%s",&gpio,arg)!=2)
55                       goto errxit;
56                   if ( *arg == 'n' )
57                       p = -1;
58                   else if ( *arg == ' l ' || *arg == 'h ' )
59                       p = *arg == 'h ' ? 1 : 0;
60                   else goto errxit;
61                   if ( gpio < 0 || gpio > 31 ) {
62                       fprintf(stderr,"%s : GPIO must be <= 31\n",
63                           argv[x]) ;
64                       return 1;
65                   }
66                   gpio_setpullup(gpio, p);
67           }
68           return 0;
69
70   errxit: fprintf(stderr,
                   "Argument '%s' must be in the form\n"
71               " <gpio>=<arg> where arg is h, l or n.\ n",
72               argv [ x ] ) ;
73           return 1;
74   }
75
76   /* End pullup.c */
```

The default drive strengths after booting are listed next, along with the GPIO addresses for the corresponding GPIO pads:

Address	GPIO Pads	Reset Drive Strength
0x2010002C	GPIO 0 to 27	8 mA
0x20100030	GPIO 28 to 45	16 mA
0x20100034	GPIO 46 to 53	8 mA

Table 10-3 summarizes the GPIO Pads Control register. Note that to be successful setting values in this register, the field labeled PASSWRD must receive the value 0x5A. This is a simple measure to avoid having the values trashed by an accidental write to this location.

Table 10-3. *GPIO Pads Control*

Bits	Field	Description		I/O	Reset
31:24	PASSWRD	0x5A	Must be 0x5A when writing	W	0x00
23:05	Reserved	0x00	Write as zero, read as don't care	R/W	
04:04	SLEW	Slew rate			
		0	Slew rate limited	R/W	1
		1	Slew rate not limited		
03:03	HYST	Enable input hysterisis			
		0	Disabled	R/W	1
		1	Enabled		
02:00	DRIVE	Drive strength		R/W	3
		0	2 mA		
		1	4 mA		
		2	6 mA		
		3	8 mA (default except 28 to 45)		
		4	10 mA		
		5	12 mA		
		6	14 mA		
		7	16 mA (GPIO 28 to 45)		

Testing Pull-up State

If you want to test the state of the pull-up resistors, the following procedure can be used:

1. Make sure no connection is attached so that the input can float.

2. Configure the GPIO pin as an input.

3. Configure the GPIO as active high (that is, not *active low*).

4. Read the input value.

    a. A reading of 1 means that the input was pulled high.

    b. A reading of 0 means that the input was pulled low.

Note that GPIO pins 2 and 3 are pulled up by external resistors, while others may be connected to other circuits (GPIO 6). This will affect your readings for those pins. Note also that pins configured for alternate functions may be *outputs* and will be driven.

When the input GPIO is configured with no pull-up, you *might* see random values, but this is unreliable. An input voltage can float above or below a threshold and remain there for a time.

The script presented in the "GPIO Input Test" section can be used to test a GPIO input (^C to exit the script).

Logic Levels

GPIO pins use 3 V logic levels. The precise BCM2835 SoC logic-level specifications are as follows:

Parameter	Volts	Description
V_{IL}	≤ 0.8	Voltage, input low
V_{IH}	≥ 1.3	Voltage, input high

As we work through several projects in this book, we'll be making frequent references to these parameters. You might want to commit these voltage levels to memory or mark the page with a tab. The voltage levels between V_{IL} and V_{IH} are considered to be ambiguous or undefined, and must be avoided.

Drive Strength

How much drive can a GPIO pin provide in terms of current drive? The design of the SoC is such that each GPIO pin can safely sink or source up to 16 mA without causing it harm.[28] The drive strength is also software configurable from 2 mA up to 16 mA.[29] The boot-up default is to use the drive strength of 8 mA.[28] However, as our test program pads.c will show, the GPIO outputs 28 to 45 were found configured for 16 mA (GPIO 28 to 31 are available on header P5).

Table 10-3 shows the SoC registers for reading and configuring the drive strength of the GPIO pins. There are three registers, affecting GPIO pins in three groups of 28 (two groups affect user-accessible GPIOs). The slew rate, hysteresis, and drive strength settings all apply at the group level. The drive strength is configured through a 3-bit value from 2 mA to 16 mA, in increments of 2 mA. When writing to these registers, the field PASSWRD must contain the hexadecimal value 0x5A, as a guard against accidental changes.

To visualize how the Raspberry Pi controls drive strength, examine Figure 10-3. The control lines Drive0 through Drive2 are enabled by bits in the DRIVE register. With these three control lines disabled (zero), only the bottom 2 mA amplifier is active (this amplifier is always enabled for outputs). This represents the weakest drive-strength setting.

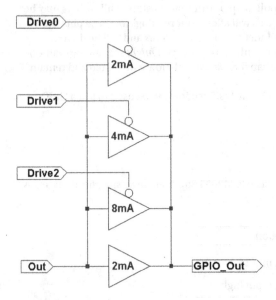

Figure 10-3. *Drive-strength control*

With Drive0 set to a 1, the top amplifier is enabled, adding another 2 mA of drive, for a total of 4 mA. Enabling Drive1 adds a further 4 mA of drive, totaling 8 mA. Enabling Drive2 brings the total drive capability to 16 mA.

It should be mentioned that these drive capabilities are *not current limiters* in any way. What they do is apply more amplifier drive in order to meet the logic-level requirements (next section). If the GPIO output is wired up to a light load like a CMOS chip or MOSFET transistor where little current is drawn, then the minimum drive of 2 mA suffices. The single GPIO 2 mA buffer can effortlessly establish a logic high in its proper voltage range as well as bring the voltage to a logic low when required.

When the GPIO output is loaded with a higher current load, the single 2 mA buffer may not be enough to keep the logic level within spec. By applying more amplifier drive, the output voltage levels are coerced into the correct operating range.

Input Pins

A GPIO input pin should experience voltages only between 0 and the 3.3 V maximum. Always exercise caution when interfacing to other circuits that use higher voltages like TTL logic, where 5 V is used. The SoC is not tolerant of overvoltages and can be damaged.

While there exist protection diodes for protecting against negative input swings, these are weak and intended only to bleed away negative static charges. Be sure to design your input circuits so that the GPIO input never sees a negative input potential.

Output Pins

As an output GPIO pin, the user bears full responsibility for current limiting. There is *no* current limiting provided. When the output pin is in the high state, as a voltage source, it tries to supply 3.3 V (within the limits of the transistor).

If this output is shorted to ground (worst case), then as much current as can be supplied will flow. This will lead to permanent damage.

The outputs also work to the specifications listed earlier, but the attached load can skew the operating voltage range. An output pin can *source* or *sink* current. The amount of current required and the amount of *output drive* configured alters the operating voltage profile. As long as you keep within the current limits for the configured drive capability, the voltage specifications should be met.

Figure 10-4 illustrates how a GPIO port sources current into its load (R_{load}). Current flows from the +3.3 V supply, through transistor M_1, out the GPIO pin, and into R_{load} to ground. Because of this, it takes a high (logic 1) to send current into the load. This makes the circuit an "active high" configuration.

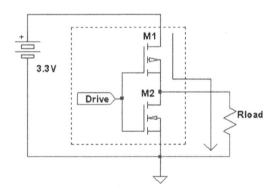

Figure 10-4. *GPIO output high*

Figure 10-5 shows how the GPIO output sinks current instead. Because R_{load} is connected to the +3.3 V supply, current flows through R_{load}, into the GPIO output pin, and through the bottom transistor M_2 to ground. To send current through the load, a low (logic 0) is written to the output port. This is the *active low* configuration.

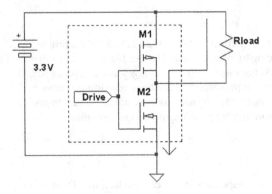

Figure 10-5. *GPIO output low*

Figure 10-6 shows the active high configuration's R_{load} circuit element substituted with an *LED* and limiting resistor *R*. Since there is no current limiting provided by the GPIO port, resistor *R* must be provided to do this.

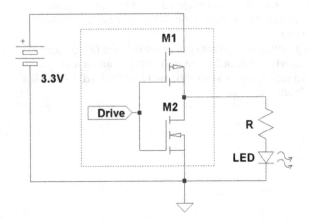

Figure 10-6. *GPIO driving an LED*

Driving LEDs

When an LED is hooked up to the GPIO output port, R_{load} becomes the LED and *the limiting resistor* (in series). The math is complicated slightly by the fact that the LED is a diode. As a diode, it has a voltage drop, which should be subtracted from the supply voltage. For red LEDs, the voltage drop is usually between 1.63 and 2.03 V.[30]

Knowing the current draw you want for the LED, the resistor R can be calculated from the following:

$$R = \frac{V_{CC} - V_{LED}}{I_{LED}}$$

where

V_{CC} is the supply voltage (+3.3 V).

V_{LED} is the voltage drop for the LED.

I_{LED} is the required current draw for the LED.

For V_{LED} it is best to assume the worst case and assume the lower voltage drop of 1.63 V. Assuming we need 8 mA to get reasonable brightness from the LED, we can calculate the resistance of the limiting resistor:

$$R = \frac{3.3 - 1.63}{0.008}$$
$$= 208.75\Omega$$

Since resistors come in standard values, we round up to a standard 10% component of 220 Ω.

■ **Note** Rounding resistance down would lead to higher current. It is better to err on the side of less current.

The LED and the 220 Ω limiting resistor can be wired according to Figure 10-4 (and shown in Figure 10-6). When wired this way, a high is written to the GPIO output port to make current flow through the LED.

The sense of the GPIO port can be altered by the sysfs file active_low (see Table 10-5 later in this chapter). Putting the GPIO pin 7 into active low mode reverses the logic sense, as follows:

```
# echo 1  >/sys/class/gpio/gpio7/active_low
```

With this mode in effect, writing a 1 to GPIO pin 7 causes the pin to go "low" on the output and causes the LED to go off:

```
# echo 1  >/sys/class/gpio/gpio7/value
```

If the LED was wired according to Figure 10-5, it would turn on instead.

Driving Logic Interfaces

For LEDs, the requirements of the interface are rather simple. The interface is a success if the LED is lit when the output port is in one state, and the LED is dark in the other. The precise voltage appearing at the GPIO output pin in these two states is of little concern, as long as the maximum current limits are respected.

When interfacing to logic, the output *voltage* is critical. For the receiving logic, the output level must be at least V_{IH} to reliably register a 1 bit (for the BCM2835, this is 1.3 V). Likewise, the output should present less than V_{IL} to reliably register a 0 in the receiver (for the BCM2835, this is 0.8V). Any voltage level between these limits is *ambiguous* and can cause the receiver to randomly see a 0 or a 1.

There are a fairly large number of approaches to interfacing between different logic families. A good source of information is provided by the document "Microchip 3V Tips 'n Tricks."[31]

Another document titled "Interfacing 3V and 5V Applications, AN240" describes the issues and challenges of interfacing between systems.[32] It describes, for example, how a 5 V system can end up raising the 3 V supply voltage if precautions are not taken.

Approaches to interfacing include direct connections (when safe), voltage-dividing resistors, diode resistor networks, and the more-complex op-amp comparators.

When choosing an approach, remember to consider the necessary switching speed of the interface required.

Driving Bi-color LEDs

This is a good point to inject a note about driving bi-color LEDs. Some of these are configured so that one LED is forward biased while the other is reversed biased. This has the advantage of needing only the usual two LED leads. To change colors, you simply change the polarity of the power going into the pair.

To drive these and choose a color, you need a way to reverse the current. This is normally done using the H-Bridge driver, which is explored in Chapter 7 of *Experimenting with Raspberry Pi* (Apress, 2014). There a bipolar stepper motor is driven by the H-Bridge driver. The LED, however, requires considerably less current, and so this is an easy assignment. If you choose a bi-color LED requiring 10 mA or less, you can drive it directly from a pair of GPIO outputs.

Figure 10-7 illustrates the bi-color LED driving arrangement. Compare this configuration with the H-Bridge in Figure 7-1 in Chapter 7 of *Experimenting with Raspberry Pi* (Apress, 2014). Do you see the similarity?

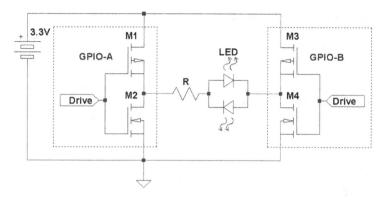

Figure 10-7. *Driving a bi-colored LED*

The pair of GPIO outputs form an H-Bridge because each of the outputs themselves are a pair of CMOS driving transistors—an upper and lower half. It is this pairing that makes them capable of both sourcing and sinking a current. By using two GPIO outputs, you form an H-Bridge driver.

To light the bi-color LED in one color, make one GPIO high (source), while the other is made low (sink). Then the current will flow through the LED from the first GPIO output into the second. To reverse the current and see the other color, make the first GPIO low and the other high. Now the current flows from the second GPIO output into the first.

Testing Drive Strength

There's nothing like finding out for yourself the configured parameters of your Raspberry Pi. The program pads.c (next) dumps out the GPIO Pads Control registers so that you can verify the actual parameters in effect.

Each GPIO pin defaults to setting 3 (for 8 mA).[28] Running the pads.c program on my Rev 2.0 Raspberry Pi showed that the GPIO group from 28 to 45 was configured for *16 mA*. GPIO pins 28 to 31 are available on header P5.

The following example session shows the output for my Raspberry Pi:

```
$ sudo ./pads
07E1002C  :    0000001B  1  1  3
07E10030  :    0000001F  1  1  7
07E10034  :    0000001B  1  1  3
```

The last four fields on each output line are as follows:

1. The word value in hexadecimal

2. The configured slew rate setting

3. The configured hysteresis setting

4. The drive-level code

135

What this suggests is that GPIO 28 through 31 could be used, if you have higher current driving requirements.

If you have a requirement to change these settings from within a C program, the program pads.c can be easily modified. Use the macro GETPAD32 (line 16) for inspiration.

```
1   /*****************************************************************
2    * pads . c : Examine GPIO Pads Control
3    *****************************************************************/
4   #include <stdio.h>
5   #include <stdlib.h>
6   #include <fcntl.h>
7   #include <sys/mman.h>
8   #include <unistd.h>
9
10  #define BCM2708_PERI_BASE 0x20000000
11  #define PADS_GPIO_BASE      (BCM2708_PERI_BASE+0x100000)
12  #define PADS_GPIO_00_27     0x002C
13  #define PADS_GPIO_28_45     0x0030
14  #define PADS_GPIO_46_53     0x0034
15
16  #define GETPAD32(offset) \
            ( *(unsigned *) ((char *) (pads)+offset))
17
18  #define BLOCK_SIZE   (4*1024)
19
20  volatile unsigned *pads ;
21
22  void
23  initialize(void)  {
24      int mem_fd = open("/dev/mem",O_RDWR|O_SYNC);
25      char *pads_map;
26
27      if ( mem_fd <= 0 ) {
28          perror("Opening/dev/mem");
29          exit(1);
30      }
31
32      pads_map = (char *)mmap(
33          NULL,                       /* Any address */
34          BLOCK_SIZE,          /* Map length */
35          PROT_READ|PROT_WRITE,
36          MAP_SHARED,
37          mem_fd,                     /* File to map */
38          PADS_GPIO_BASE  /* Offset to registers */
39      );
40
41      if ( (long)pads_map == -1L ) {
42          perror("mmap failed.");
```

```
43          exit(1);
44      }
45
46      close(mem_fd);
47      pads = (volatile unsigned *)pads_map;
48  }
49
50  int
51  main(int argc,char **argv) {
52      int x;
53      union {
54          struct {
55              unsigned    drive : 3;
56              unsigned    hyst  : 1;
57              unsigned    slew : 1;
58              unsigned    reserved : 13;
59              unsigned    passwrd  : 8;
60          } s;
61          unsigned  w;
62      } word;
63
64      initialize();
65
66      for ( x=PADS_GPIO_00_27; x<=PADS_GPIO_46_53; x += 4 ) {
67          word.w = GETPAD32(x) ;
68          printf("%08X : %08X %x %x %x\n" ,
69              x+0x7E10000, word.w,
70              word.s.slew, word.s. hyst, word.s.drive) ;
71      }
72
73      return 0;
74  }
75
76  /* End */
```

GPIO Current Budget

Gert van Loo states that "the Raspberry-Pi 3V3 supply was designed with a maximum current of ~3 mA per GPIO pin."[29] He correctly concludes that if "you load each pin with 16 mA, the total current is 272 mA."

From this, we can calculate the designed current budget for GPIO pins:

1. Gert is referring to 17 GPIO pins ($\dfrac{272mA}{16mA} = 17$)

2. The Pi is designed for $17 \times 3 \ mA = 51 mA$

This is consistent with the 50 mA capacity figure we arrived at in Chapter 2. This is the remaining current capacity available from pins P1-01, P1-17, and P5-02.

Consequently, when budgeting your 3.3 V supply current, factor in the following:

GPIO: Current used for each GPIO *output* pin assigned (2 mA to 16 mA)

+3.3 V: All current going to circuits powered from P1-01, P1-17, and P5-02.

MAX232CSE: If you attached a RS-232 adapter, allow for about 15 mA.

To save on your power budget, configure unused GPIO pins as inputs.

Configuration

Each GPIO pin is affected by several configuration choices:

- General-purpose input, output, or alternate function
- Input event detection method
- Input pull-up/pull-down resistors
- Output drive level

Alternate Function Select

When a GPIO pin is configured, you must choose whether it is an input, an output, or an alternate function (like the UART). The complete list of choices is shown in Table 10-4. The exact nature of what *alternate function x* means depends on the pin being configured.

Table 10-4. *Alternate Function Selection*

Code	Function Selected	ALT
000	GPIO pin is an input.	
001	GPIO pin is an output.	
100	GPIO pin is alternate function 0.	0
101	GPIO pin is alternate function 1.	1
110	GPIO pin is alternate function 2.	2
111	GPIO pin is alternate function 3.	3
011	GPIO pin is alternate function 4.	4
010	GPIO pin is alternate function 5.	5

The values shown in the table's Code column are used in the configuration register itself. The alternate function numbers are listed in the ALT column. Keeping these two straight can be confusing when programming. Once the function has been selected, the configuration is then fine-tuned according to its peripheral type.

Output Pins

When a pin is configured for output, the remaining elements of configuration consist of the following:

- Logic sense
- Output state

The output state of the GPIO pins can either be set by the kernel as a 32-bit word (affects 32 GPIOs at a time) or individually set or cleared. Having individual set/clear operations allows the host to change individual bits without disturbing the state of others (or having to know their state).

Input Pins

Input pins are more complex because of the additional hardware functionality offered. This requires that the input GPIO pin be configured for the following:

- Detect rising input signals (synchronous/asynchronous)
- Detect falling input signals (synchronous/asynchronous)
- Detect high-level signals
- Detect low-level signals
- Logic sense
- Interrupt handling (handled by driver)
- Choose no pull-up; use a pull-up or pull-down resistor

Once these choices have been made, it is possible to receive data related to input signal changes, or simply query the pin's current state.

Alternate Function

When an alternate function such as the UART is chosen, many aspects of the pin's configuration are predetermined. Despite this, each pin used by the peripheral should be preconfigured for input or output according to its function. These details are normally provided by the supporting driver.

Sysfs GPIO Access

In this section, we're going to access the GPIO pins through the /sys pseudo file system. This is the GPIO *driver* interface. Because it provides file system objects, it is possible to control GPIO pins from the command line (or shell).

The C/C++ programmer might be quick to dismiss this approach, because it might seem too slow. However, for input pins, the driver provides the advantage of providing a reasonable edge-level detection that is not possible when accessing the GPIO registers directly. The driver is able to receive interrupts when a GPIO state changes. This information can in turn be passed onto the application program using poll(2) or select(2).

Everything that you need for GPIO access is rooted in the top-level directory:

```
/sys/class/gpio
```

At this directory level, two main control pseudo files are maintained by the driver. These are write-only:

> export: Requests the kernel to export control of the requested GPIO pin by writing its number to the file
>
> unexport: Relinquishes control of the GPIO pin by writing its number to the file

---

■ **Note** Even root gets the permission denied if you try to read these files.

Normally, the kernel manages the GPIO pins, especially if they are used for resources that need them (like the UART). In order for an application to manipulate a GPIO pin, it must first request that the kernel relinquish control of the requested pin. From a userspace perspective, the operation is like opening a file. The script or program should be prepared for failure in the event that a GPIO pin is busy.

CORRECT USE OF SUDO

It is tempting to perform some operations from a nonroot account, using sudo like this:

```
$ sudo echo 17 >/sys/class/gpio/export
-bash: /sys/class/gpio/export: Permission denied
```

This does not work because the I/O redirection is performed by the shell *before* the sudo command begins. Change to interactive mode first and then the operation will succeed:

```
$ sudo -i
# echo 17 >/sys/class/gpio/export
```

export

The `export` pseudo file allows you to request a GPIO pin from the kernel. For example, if you want to manipulate GPIO pin 17, you request it from the kernel by writing its pin number to the pseudo file:

```
$ sudo -i
# echo 17 >/sys/class/gpio/export
```

After a successful run, list the directory /sys/class/gpio:

```
# ls
export  gpio17  gpiochip0  unexport
#
```

A new subdirectory (a symlink to a directory, actually) named gpio17 appears. This tells you that the kernel has given up control of GPIO 17 and has provided you this file system object to manipulate. At this point, you can consider the GPIO 17 as available.

unexport

Some applications may require a GPIO pin for only a short time. When the application is finished with the pin, the application can release the pin back to the kernel. This is done by writing to the unexport pseudo file:

```
$ sudo  -i
# echo  17  >/sys/class/gpio/unexport
```

After this command completes, the pseudo object gpio17 disappears from the /sys/class/gpio directory. This confirms that the GPIO is now being managed by the driver and makes it impossible for userspace programs to mess with it (except for direct register access).

gpioX

Once you have a file system object like /sys/class/gpio/gpio17 to work with, you can configure it and perform I/O. The main objects that you'll see are outlined in Table 10-5. The ones normally used by shell programs are simply as follows:

> direction: To set the I/O direction
>
> value: To read or write the I/O bit
>
> active_low: To alter the sense of logic

Table 10-5. */sys/class/gpio/gpioX Objects*

Object	Type	R/W	Values	Description
direction	File	R/W	in	Input pin
			out	Output pin
			high	Output & high
			low	Output & low
value	File	R/W	0 or 1	Read or write
edge	File	R/W	None	No edge
			Rising	Rising edge
			Falling	Falling edge
			Both	Rising or falling
active_low	File	R/W	0	Normal sense
			1	Active low
uevent	File			
subsystem	Symlink			Symlink to self
power	Directory	R		

The values used for direction are worth expanding on:

Value	Description
in	GPIO becomes an input port.
out	GPIO becomes an output port (with some prior state).
high	GPIO becomes output, but in a 1 state (high).
low	GPIO becomes output, but in a 0 state (low).

The high and low options look like convenience frills, but they're not. Consider configuring an output and setting it to 1:

```
# echo out >/sys/class/gpio/gpio7/direction
# echo 1 >/sys/class/gpio/gpio7/value
```

Some time will pass before the execution of the second command takes place to establish the correct output level. If the GPIO output state was previously left in a zero state, the GPIO 7 pin will reflect a 0 (low) until the second command completes. For electronic devices operating in nanosecond time frames, this can be a problem.

To provide glitch-free configuration, the following can be done instead:

```
# echo high >/sys/class/gpio/gpio7/direction
```

This way, the driver takes the necessary steps to establish the correct output level prior to making the pin an output.

The settings of the file named edge affect how a C program (for example) would process poll(2) on the file named value (reading). A poll(2) system call could block the execution of the program until the required event occurred (like a rising edge).

Active Low

Sometimes it is desirable to have the logic inverted for the GPIO pin being used. For example, when driving an LED in the circuit configuration of Figure 10-5, a logic low is required to light the LED.

Value	Description
0	Noninverted logic
1	Inverted logic

Inverting the logic allows you to light the LED with a logic 1:

```
# echo 1 >/sys/class/gpio/gpio7/active_low
# echo 1 >/sys/class/gpio/gpio7/value
```

Conversely, if you don't want inverted logic, you should be certain to establish that by writing a 0:

```
# echo 0 >/sys/class/gpio/gpio7/active_low
```

Chip Level

You will also notice the presence of a subdirectory named gpiochipN in /sys/class/gpio, where *N* is a numeric digit. The following main pseudo files exist within that directory:

> base: The value read should be the same value *N*, which is the first GPIO managed by this chip.

> label: The label (for example, bcm2708_gpio) of the chip, which is not necessarily unique. Used for diagnostic purposes.

> ngpio: The value read indicates how many GPIOs this chip manages, starting with the value read from base.

GPIO Tester

If you decided to build yourself a prototype board with the Raspberry Pi mounted on it, you may find this simple shell script useful for checking the wiring of the GPIO breakout clips. Or perhaps you just want to verify that the connection brought out to the breadboard is the correct one. Simply supply the GPIO pin number that you want to blink, on the command line:

```
$ cat ./gp
#!/bin/bash

GPIO="$1"
SYS=/sys/class/gpio
DEV=/sys/class/gpio/gpio$GPIO

if [ ! -d $DEV ] ; then
    # Make pin visible
    echo $GPIO >$SYS/export
fi

# Set pin to output
echo out >$DEV/direction

function put() {
    # Set value of pin (1 or 0)
    echo $1 >$DEV/value
}

while true ; do
    put 1
    echo "GPIO $GPIO: on"
    sleep 1
    put 0
    echo "GPIO $GPIO: off $(date)"
    sleep 1
done

# End
```

To exercise GPIO 25 (GEN6), use this command (project file scripts/gp):

```
# ./gp 25
```

When testing with an LED and alligator clip lead, ground yourself to the ground pin first (or better still, a good ground like a water tap). Static electricity can be especially bad in the winter months. It not only can cause your Pi to reset but also can inflict internal damage. After discharging yourself to the ground pin, apply the lead and allow time enough for 1-second-on and 1-second-off events.

■ **Note**   Cats are especially bad for static electricity.

GPIO Input Test

To test out the GPIO input capability, a simple script is presented next (and is available in the scripts subdirectory as a file named input). By default, it assumes 0 for the *active low* setting, meaning that normal logic applies to the input values. If, on the other hand, a 1 is used, inverted logic will be applied. Using the script named input, apply one of the following commands to start it (^C to end it):

```
# ./input 0    # Normal "active high" logic
. . .
# ./input 1    # Use active low logic
```

The script, of course, can be modified, but as listed, it reads an input on GPIO 25 (GEN6) and presents what it has read to GPIO 24 (GEN5). It additionally reports what has been read to standard output. If the output (GPIO 24) is wired to an LED, the input status will be visible in the LED (use Figure 10-6 as a guide for wiring).

The script has its limitations, one of which is that the sleep(1) command is used. This causes it to have a somewhat sluggish response. If you don't like that, you can comment out the else and sleep commands. As a consequence, it will hog the CPU, however, but be more responsive.

```
#!/bin/bash

ALO="${1:-0}"  # 1=active low, else 0
INP=25         # Read from GPIO 25 (GEN6)
OUT=24         # Write t o GPIO 24 (GEN5)

set -eu
trap "close_all" 0

function close_all() {
  close $INP
  close $OUT
}
function open() { # pin direction
  dev=$SYS/gpio$1
  if [ ! -d $dev ] ; then
    echo $1 >$SYS/export
  fi
  echo $2 >$dev/direction
  echo none >$dev/edge
  echo $ALO >$dev/active_low
}
```

```
function close() { # pin
  echo $1 >$SYS/unexport
}
function put() { # pin value
  echo $2 >$SYS/gpio$1/value
}
function get() { # pin
  read BIT <$SYS/gpio$1/value
  echo $BIT
}
count=0
SYS=/sys/class/gpio

open $INP in
open $OUT out
put $OUT 1
LBIT=2

while true ; do
  RBIT=$(get $INP)
  if [ $RBIT -ne $LBIT ] ; then
    put $OUT $RBIT
    printf "%04d Status : %d\n" $count $RBIT
    LBIT=$RBIT
    let count=count+1
  else
    sleep 1
  fi
done

# End
```

The following is an example session:

```
# ./input
0000 Status : 0
0001 Status : 1
0002 Status : 0
0003 Status : 1
^C
#
```

When GPIO 25 is grounded, 0 should be read, as reported in line 0000 of the example. If you then apply a high (for example, from the +3.3 V supply), a 1 should be reported.

Floating Potentials

The beginning student may be puzzled about "glitches" seen by some GPIO inputs (28 or 29). When a GPIO input without a pull-up resistor is unattached, the line can "float," or change over time, due to static electrical buildup. Unless a pull-up or pull-down resistor is attached (or configured), the pin can assume *intermediate* voltages. A voltage in the range of $V_{IL} = 0.8\ V$ to $V_{IH} = 1.3\ V$ is ambiguous to the Pi. Input voltages in this range may read randomly as 1s or 0s.

■ **Caution** If you are using a loose wire or alligator clip to apply high or low signals to an input GPIO pin, be very careful to avoid static electricity, which can cause damage. Use a ground strap or hold onto the Pi's ground to bleed any static away, while changing connections. Static electricity may also cause your Raspberry Pi to reset. A real ground, like a water tap, is best for bleeding off static.

When using a button or switch, for example, use a pull-up resistor to +3.3 V (or configure the SoC to use one). In this manner, high is immediately seen by the input when the switch or button is temporarily unconnected.

■ **Note** A switch is temporarily disconnected while changing its poles.

Reading Events

One of the shortcomings of the input script is that it must poll the input pin's value continuously, to see if the value has changed. In a multiprocessing environment like Linux, it is rude to burn the CPU like this (hence the compromise with the sleep command). A better design would have the program wait for a change on the input pin, allowing other processes to use the CPU while it waits.

The GPIO driver within the kernel is, in fact, able to do that, though not usable by shell commands. The C program evinput.c is an example program that takes advantage of this capability and is presented next. It uses the poll(2) system call to accomplish this. The basic procedure used is this:

1. The GPIO pin X is configured for input.

2. The value of /sys/class/gpio/gpioX/edge has been configured for the edge(s) to be reported (see Table 10-5).

3. When querying the input pin, the open file descriptor for / sys/class/gpio/gpioX/value is provided to the poll(2) call (line 111).

4. The time-out is specified as –1 in argument 3, so poll(2) will wait forever, if necessary.

5. When there is new data for the GPIO input, poll(2) returns and rc will be greater than zero, breaking out of the loop.

6. The program must rewind to the beginning of the pseudo file with lseek(2) (line 118).

7. Finally, the text is read from the value file in line 119.

Step 6 can be omitted if you only need notification. However, to read the correct data, a rewind to the start of the pseudo file is required.

The program shown also checks whether the signal handler was called. If it sees that variable is_signaled has been set, the routine gpio_poll() returns –1 to indicate to the caller that a program exit is needed (lines 112 to 113).

Test Run

A test was performed using a GPIO output pin (27) wired to the input pin (17). In one session, GPIO output pin 27 was changed from 0 to 1 and back. The events were captured in the other session, running ./evinput.

■ **Note**   If the reader compiles the programs using the included makefile for each program, the programs are automatically built to use setuid root. Doing this allows them to run with root privileges, without needing to use the sudo command.

The following is a session output obtained from the ./evinput run. The output pauses after reporting the first line (line 4). Following that, new lines appear whenever the input pins change state.

```
1 $ ./evinput 17
2 Monitoring for GPIO input changes:
3
4 GPIO 17 changed: 0
5 GPIO 17 changed: 1
6 GPIO 17 changed: 0
7 GPIO 17 changed: 1
8 ^C
9 $
```

Input GPIO pin 17 was changed from this separate session, using output GPIO 27 (recall that it is wired to GPIO 17 for this test):

```
1  # cd /sys/class/gpio
2  # echo 27 >export
3  # ls
4  export gpio27 gpiochip0 unexport
5  # cd gpio27
6  # ls
7  active_low direction edge power subsystem uevent value
8  # echo out >direction
9  # echo 0 >value
10 # # s t a r t e d . / evinput 17 he r e . . .
11 # echo 1 >value
12 # echo 0 >value
13 # echo 1 >value
```

From the sessions shown, GPIO 17 was set low in the preceding line 9. After that, the ./evinput program was started and the first line is reported (line 4 in the evinput session). As the input pin changed state in lines 11+ (in the preceding code), the input events were being reported in lines 5+ (evinput session).

Checking the system with the top command, you'll see that ./evinput does not consume CPU. Yet the program is indeed responsive to the input change events. This leaves the CPU for all of your other processes that you may need to run.

```
1   / ****************************************************************
2   *  evinput.c : Event driven GPIO input
3   *
4   * ./evinput gpio#
5   *****************************************************************/
6
7   #include <stdio.h>
8   #include <stdlib.h>
9   #include <fcntl.h>
10  #include <unistd.h>
11  #include <string.h>
12  #include <errno.h>
13  #include <signal.h>
14  #include <assert.h>
15  #include <sys/poll.h>
16
17  static int gpio_inpin = -1; /* GPIO input pin */
18  static int is_signaled = 0; /* Exit program if signaled */
19
20  typedef enum {
21          gp_export=0,        /* /sys/class/gpio/export */
22          gp_unexport,        /* /sys/class/gpio/unexport */
23          gp_direction,       /* /sys/class/gpio%d/direction */
```

```
24            gp_edge,          /* /sys/class/gpio%d/edge */
25            gp_value          /* /sys/class/gpio%d/value */
26  } gpio_path_t;
27
28  /*
29   * Internal : Create a pathname for type in buf.
30   * /
31  static const char *
32  gpio_setpath(int pin, gpio_path_t type, char *buf,
        unsigned bufsiz) {
33          static const char * paths[] = {
34                  "export", "unexport", "gpio%d/direction",
35                  "gpio%d/edge", "gpio%d/value"};
36          int slen;
37
38          strncpy (buf, "/sys/class/gpio/", bufsiz);
39          bufsiz -= (slen = strlen(buf));
40          snprintf(buf+slen, bufsiz, paths[type], pin);
41          return buf;
42  }
43
44  /*
45   * Open /sys/class/gpio%d/value for edge detection :
46   */
47  static int
48  gpio_open_edge(int pin, const char * edge)  {
49          char buf [128];
50          FILE *f;
51          int fd;
52
53          /* Export pin : /sys/class/gpio/export */
54          gpio_setpath(pin, gp_export, buf, size of buf);
55          f = fopen(buf, "w");
56          assert(f);
57          fprintf(f,"%d\n", pin);
58          fclose(f);
59
60          /* Direction :  /sys/class/gpio%d/direction */
61          gpio_setpath(pin, gp_direction, buf, size of buf);
62          f = fopen(buf, "w");
63          assert(f);
64          fprintf(f,"in\n");
65          fclose(f);
66
67          /* Edge :  /sys/class/gpio%d/edge */
68          gpio_setpath(pin, gp_edge, buf, size of buf);
69          f = fopen (buf, "w");
```

```
70          assert(f);
71          fprintf(f,"% s\n", edge);
72          fclose(f);
73
74          /* Value :   /sys/class/gpio%d/value */
75          gpio_setpath(pin, gp_value, buf, size of buf);
76          fd = open(buf,O_RDWR);
77          return fd;
78  }
79
80  /*
81   *  Close (unexport) GPIO pin :
82   * /
83  static void
84  gpio_close(int pin) {
85          char buf[128];
86          FILE *f;
87
88          / * Unexport :   /sys/class/gpio/unexport */
89          gpio_setpath(pin, gp_unexport, buf, size of buf);
90          f = fopen(buf, "w");
91          assert(f);
92          fprintf(f,"%d\n", pin);
93          fclose(f);
94  }
95
96  /*
97   * This routine will block until the open GPIO pin has changed
98   * value. This pin should be connected to the MCP23017 /INTA
99   * pin.
100 */
101 static int
102 gpio_poll(int fd) {
103         struct pollfd polls;
104         char buf [32];
105         int rc, n;
106
107         polls.fd = fd;   /* /sys/class/gpio17/value */
108         polls.events = POLLPRI;     /* Exceptions */
109
110         do     {
111                 rc = poll(&polls, 1, -1); /* Block */
112                 if ( is_signaled )
113                         return -1; /* Exit if ^C received */
114         } while (   rc < 0 && errno == EINTR );
115
116         assert (rc > 0);
117
```

151

```
118             lseek(fd, 0, SEEK_SET);
119             n = read(fd, buf, size of buf);      /* Read value */
120             assert(n > 0);
121             buf[n] = 0;
122
123             rc = sscanf(buf,"% d",&n);
124             assert(rc==1);
125             return n;   /* Return value */
126 }
127
128 /*
129  * Signal handler to quit the program  :
130  * /
131 static void
132 sigint_handler(int signo) {
133             is_signaled = 1; /* Signal to exit program */
134 }
135
136 /*
137  * Main program :
138  */
139 int
140 main(int argc, char ** argv)  {
141             int fd, v;
142
143             /*
144              * Get GPIO input pin to use :
145              */
146             if (argc != 2) {
147 usage:       fprintf(stderr,"Usage: %s <gpio_in_pin>\n",
                    argv[0]);
148                 return 1;
149             }
150             if ( sscanf(argv[1], "%d",&gpio_inpin) != 1 )
151                     goto usage;
152             if ( gpio_inpin < 0 || gpio_inpin >= 32 )
153                     goto usage;
154
155             signal(SIGINT,sigint_handler); /* Trap on SIGINT */
156             fd = gpio_open_edge(gpio_inpin,"both");
157
158             puts("Monitoring for GPIO input changes: \n");
159
160             while ((v=gpio_poll(fd)) >= 0 ) {
                    /* Block until input changes */
161                 printf("GPIO %d changed: %d\n",gpio_inpin,
                        v);
162             } while ( !is_signaled ); /* Quit if ^C' d */
163
```

```
164        putchar('\n');
165        close(fd);              /* Close gpio%d/value */
166        gpio_close(gpio_inpin); /* Unexport gpio */
167        return 0;
168 }
169
170 /*  End event.c */
```

Direct Register Access

It is possible to access the GPIO registers directly. The module gpio_io.c shows the code that can be used for this. It requires the program to invoke gpio_init() upon startup, which then makes the registers available. The code as presented is intended to be #included into the module using it. (Normally, it would be compiled as a separate module.) The API made available is outlined in the following subsections.

These routines are used in several examples and projects within this book, including the following:

> pullup: Change the pull-up register setting.
>
> bipolar: Drive a bipolar stepper motor (Chapter 7 of *Experimenting with Raspberry Pi* [Apress, 2014]).
>
> rtscts: Change the ALT function (Chapter 9).
>
> valt: View ALT function settings (subdir valt in source code).
>
> unipolar: Drive a unipolar stepper motor (Chapter 6 of *Experimenting with Raspberry Pi* [Apress, 2014]).
>
> dht11: Humidity and temperature sensor (Chapter 1 of *Experimenting with Raspberry Pi* [Apress, 2014]).
>
> pwm: Pulse width modulation (Chapter 9 of *Experimenting with Raspberry Pi* [Apress, 2014]).

gpio_init()

This function call opens access to the GPIO registers. This will require root privileges, which is why many programs in this book were compiled with setuid root. The operation of this routine is to gain access to the physical memory space, so that the GPIO registers can be accessed. This procedure is covered in the "Memory Mapping" section of Chapter 4.

```
void gpio_init(void);
```

gpio_config()

This function call allows the caller to configure a pin as input or output:

```
typedef enum {
    Input = 0,      /* GPIO is an Input */
    Output          /* GPIO is an Output */
} direction_t;

void gpio_config(int gpio,direction_t output);
```

The arguments are as follows:

gpio: The GPIO pin to be configured

output: The value Input or Output

gpio_write()

This function permits the caller to set the output GPIO pin to a 1 or a 0.

```
void gpio_write(int gpio,int bit);
```

The arguments are as follows:

gpio: The GPIO pin to write to

bit: The value of the output bit (1 or 0)

Only the least significant bit of argument bit is used.

gpio_read()

This function reads the requested GPIO pin and returns the bit (0 or 1).

```
int gpio_read(int gpio);
```

The single argument gpio is used to specify the GPIO pin to be read.

gpio_io.c

The following pages show the program listing for gpio_io.c:

```
1    /******************************************************************
2     *  gpio_io.c :      GPIO Access Code
3     ******************************************************************/
4
5    #define BCM2708_PERI_BASE 0x20000000
6    #define GPIO_BASE (BCM2708_PERI_BASE + 0x200000)
7    #define BLOCK_SIZE (4*1024)
8
9    /* GPIO setup macros. Always use INP_GPIO (x) before using OUT_GPIO(x)
10      or SET_GPIO_ALT(x, y ) */
11   #define INP_GPIO(g) \
         *(ugpio + ((g)/10)) &= ~(7 <<(((g) % 10)*3))
12   #define OUT_GPIO(g)
         *(ugpio + ((g)/10)) |=  (1 <<(((g) % 10)*3))
13   #define SET_GPIO_ALT(g,a)  \
14       *(ugpio + (((g)/10))) |= (((a) <=3?(a) + 4 : \
         (a)==4?3:2)<<(((g)%10)*3))
15
16   #define  GPIO_SET *(ugpio+7)  /* sets bits */
17   #define  GPIO_CLR *(ugpio+10) /* clears bits */
18   #define  GPIO_GET *(ugpio+13) /* gets all GPIO input levels  */
19
20   typedef enum {
21      Input = 0,        /* GPIO is an Input*/
22      Output            /* GPIO is an Output*/
23   } direction_t;
24
25   static volatile unsigned *ugpio;
26
27   /******************************************************************
28    * Perform initialization to access GPIO registers:
29    * Sets up pointer ugpio.
30    ******************************************************************/
31   static void
32   gpio_init() {
33       int fd;
34       char *map;
35       /* Needs root access */
36       fd = open("/dev/mem",O_RDWR|O_SYNC);
37       if ( fd < 0 ) {
38           perror("Opening/dev/mem");
39           exit(1);
40       }
41
```

```
42      map = (char * ) mmap(
43          NULL,                               /* Any address */
44          BLOCK_SIZE,                         /* # of bytes */
45          PROT_READ| PROT_WRITE,
46          MAP_SHARED,                         /* Shared */
47          fd,                                 /* /dev/mem */
48          GPIO_BASE                           /* Offset to GPIO */
49      );
50
51      if ( (long)map == 1L ) {
52          perror("mmap(/dev/mem)");
53          exit(1);
54      }
55
56      close(fd);
57      ugpio = (volatile unsigned *)map;
58  }
59
60  /**********************************************************************
61   * Configure GPIO as Input or Output
62   **********************************************************************/
63  static inline void
64  gpio_config (int gpio, direction_t output) {
65      INP_GPIO (gpio);
66      if ( output ) {
67          OUT_GPIO(gpio);
68      }
69  }
70
71  /**********************************************************************
72   * Write a bit to the GPIO pin
73   **********************************************************************/
74  static inline void
75  gpio_write(int gpio, int bit) {
76      unsigned sel = 1  << gpio;
77
78      if ( bit ) {
79          GPIO_SET = sel;
80      } else  {
81          GPIO_CLR = sel;
82      }
83  }
84
85  /**********************************************************************
86   * Read a bit from a GPIO pin
87   **********************************************************************/
88  static inline int
```

```
89  gpio_read(int gpio)  {
90      unsigned sel = 1 << gpio;
91
92      return (GPIO_GET) & sel ? 1 : 0 ;
93  }
94  .
95  /* End gpio_io.c */
```

GPIO Transistor Driver

The GPIO pins on the Pi are often going to be pressed into driving something in the outside world. GPIO pins 28 to 31 can drive up to 16 mA, maximum. The remaining GPIO pins are configured to drive up to 8 mA. These are fairly weak interfaces to the outside world.

Sometimes all that is needed is a simple one-transistor buffer. The 2N2222A transistor is cheap and drives a fair amount of current. Figure 10-8 shows a simple driver circuit attached to a GPIO output pin.

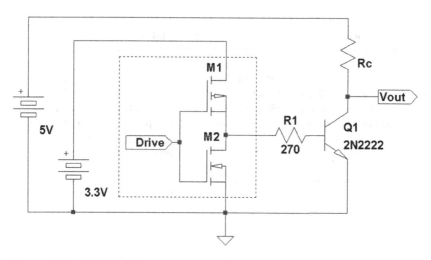

Figure 10-8. *2N2222A driver*

The GPIO output driver sees only a diode-like path to ground through the base of transistor Q_1. Resistor R_1 is chosen to limit that current.

The resistor shown as Rc in the figure represents the load, like a high-current LED in series with a current-limiting resistor. Alternatively, it may be a resistor chosen so that the *Vout* represents a stiffer output voltage.

In the diagram, the resistor R_c is connected to the +5 V power supply. This is safe because current *cannot* flow from the collector into the base of Q_1. This prevents 5 V from flowing into the GPIO pin (that junction is *reversed* biased). Thus Q_1 allows you to

157

convert the 3.3 V GPIO output into a 5 V TTL signal, for example. The 2N2222A transistor has an absolute maximum V_{CE} of 30 V. This allows you to drive even higher voltage loads, provided that you stay within the transistor's current and power ratings.

Driver Design

The transistor driver circuit is limited by the power-handling capability of Q_1 and the maximum collector current. Looking at the datasheet, the maximum power listed for Q_1 is 0.5 W at 25°C. When the transistor is turned on (saturated), the voltage across Q_1 (V_{CE}) is between 0.3 V and 1 V (see $V_{CE(sat)}$ in the datasheet). The remainder of the voltage is developed across the load. If we assume the worst case of 1 V for V_{CE} (leaving 4 V across the load), we can compute the maximum current for I_C:

$$
\begin{aligned}
I_C &= \frac{P_{Q1}}{V_{CE}} \\
&= \frac{1}{0.3} \\
&= 3.3A
\end{aligned}
$$

Clearly, this calculated current exceeds the listed absolute maximum current I_C of 600 mA. So we use the maximum current for $I_C = 600$ mA instead. For safety, we use the minimum of these maximum ratings. While this transistor is clearly capable of driving up to 600 mA of current, let's design our driver for a modest current flow of 100 mA.

The next thing to check is the H_{FE} of the part. The parameter value required is the *lowest H_{FE}* value for the amount of collector current flowing (H_{FE} drops with increasing I_C current). A STMicroelectronics datasheet shows its 2N2222A part as having an $H_{FE} = 40$, $I_C = 500$ *mA*, with $V_{CE} = 10$ *V*. They also have a more favorable H_{FE} value of 100, for 150 mA, but it is best to err on the side of safety. We can probably assume a safe compromise of $H_{FE} = 50$.

The H_{FE} parameter is important because it affects how much current is required to drive Q_1's base. The input base current is calculated as follows:

$$
\begin{aligned}
I_B &= \frac{I_C}{H_{FE}} \\
&= \frac{100mA}{50} \\
&= 2mA
\end{aligned}
$$

This value tells us that the GPIO pin will need to supply up to 2 mA of drive into Q_1's base. With 2 mA of drive, Q_1 will be able to conduct up to 100 mA in the collector circuit. A current of 2 mA is easily accommodated by any GPIO pin. Note that if you were to design closer to the design limits of this transistor (500 mA in this example), you should probably allow an additional 10% of base current "overdrive" to make certain that the transistor goes into saturation.

Current flow into the base of Q_1 creates a voltage drop of $V_{BE} = 0.7$ V, from the input base lead to ground. So to calculate the resistor value R_1 we take the V_{R1} divided by the current. The highest voltage coming from GPIO is going to be slightly less than the 3.3 V power supply rail. It is safe to assume that $GPIO_{HIGH} = 3$ V. The voltage appearing across R_1 is thus $GPIO_{HIGH} - V_{BE}$.

$$R_1 = \frac{GPIO_{HIGH} - V_{BE}}{I_B}$$
$$= \frac{3 - 0.7}{0.002}$$
$$= 1,150\Omega$$

The nearest 10% standard resistor value is $R_1 = 1.2$ $k\Omega$. Using this resistor value as a check, let's compute backward what our actual drive capability is from Q_1. First we need to recompute I_B now that we know R_1:

$$I_B = \frac{GPIO_{HIGH} - V_{BE}}{R_1}$$
$$= \frac{3 - 0.7}{1200}$$
$$= 1.9mA$$

This tells us that the GPIO output pin will not have to source more than 1.9 mA of current, using $R_1 = 1.2$ $k\Omega$. Now let's calculate the maximum drive we can reliably expect in the collector circuit of Q_1:

$$I_C = I_B \times H_{FE}$$
$$= 0.0019.50$$
$$= 95mA$$

■ **Note** This discussion glibly avoids the effects of components being within ±10% tolerance.

This computes that the designed 2N2222A driver circuit is capable of driving up to 95 mA.

To obtain even more performance out of that driver (if you need it), you could choose a resistor closer to the actual value desired (1150 Ω). It turns out that a 1% resistor can be had at exactly 1.15 $k\Omega$:

$$I_C = I_B \times H_{FE}$$
$$= 0.002.50$$
$$= 100mA$$

Be careful that your design does not stress the transistor beyond its maximum ratings (power and current). You might be willing to risk the cheap transistor, but keep in mind that the poor little thing might be holding back a higher voltage (like a river dam). If the transistor is destroyed, the high voltage may come crashing into the base circuit and cause damage to the Pi's GPIO pin. So be nice to $Q1$!

Substitution

You don't have to use my choice of the 2N2222A transistor for driving a load. Substitute what you have or what you plan to order. Today's DMMs can measure the transistor H_{FE}, so that makes planning easier when using junk box parts.

Another critical factor in selecting a part is the power capability of the transistor. You should probably know exactly what that limit is, unless you are driving an extremely light load. Finally, it is important to know what the maximum voltage ratings are for the selected transistor, if you plan to drive voltages higher than 3 V. You need to be able to count on it holding back those higher voltages in the collector circuit to prevent damage to the Pi.

Inductive Loads

Inductive loads like relays and motors present a special problem. They generate a high reverse voltage when current is switched off or interrupted. When the relay coil is turned off, the magnetic field collapses around the coil of wire. This induces a high voltage, which can damage the Pi (and can also provide a mild electric shock).

Electric motors exhibit a similar problem. As the DC current sparks and stutters at the commutator inside the motor, high reverse voltage spikes are sent back into the driving circuit. This is due to the magnetic field collapsing around the motor windings.

Consequently, inductive loads need a reverse-biased diode across the load to short out any induced currents. The diode conducts only when the back electromotive force (EMF) is generated by the inductive load.

Figure 10-9 shows diode D_1 reverse biased across the relay coil winding L_1 (or motor). The diode bleeds away any reverse current that might be generated. Use a diode with sufficient current-carrying capability (matching at least the current in Q_1).

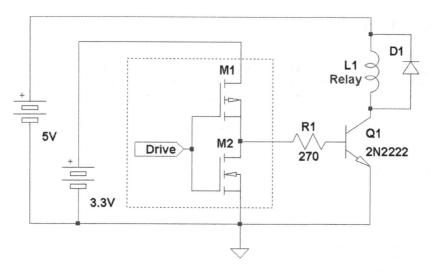

Figure 10-9. *Driver for inductive load*

Since there is no current-limiting resistor used in series with L_1, whether motor or relay, make sure that no more current than I_{Cmax} will flow. For relays, you need a coil resistance greater than or equal to 50 Ω, when driven from approximately 5 V. Otherwise, you risk burning out driver Q_1 (assuming the 2N2222A with its power limit of 0.5 watts at 5 V). You can drive lower resistance coils, if you designed your driver to handle the additional current. For example, a 500 mA driver can handle coil resistances as low as 10 ohms (at 5 V).

The 2N2222A transistor is probably suitable for only the smallest of electric motors. Depending on how it is used, a motor can stall and thus greatly increase its current demands. Motors also have high startup currents. If the motor is started and stopped frequently, the driving transistor may be overworked.

Driver Summary

This section on the transistor driver should not be thought of as your only choice in driver solutions. It was presented because it is simple and cheap and can fill the need for many small loads, like high-current LEDs or panel lightbulbs. Simple and cheap may be essential for robot building when many drivers are required.

While students may use the Gertboard for labs, we still need to provide a substitute when the Raspberry Pi is integrated into something that was built (like a robot). It might be wise to stock up on a few good transistor types for this purpose.

Utility gpio

For this book, I have avoided using instances of "magic package X." However, the wiringPi project is popular enough that no chapter on GPIO would be complete without mentioning it. The wiringPi project provides a handy utility for displaying and changing GPIO functionality. The package can be downloaded from here:

```
https://projects.drogon.net/raspberry-pi/wiringpi/download-and-install
```

This page lists instructions for obtaining, compiling, and installing the package. Once installed, the gpio command is available:

```
$ gpio -h
gpio : Usage : gpio -v
       gpio -h
       gpio [-g ] <read/write /wb/pwm/ clock/mode> ...
       gpio [-p ] <read/write /wb> ...
       gpio readall
       gpio unexportall/exports ...
       gpio export/edge/unexport ...
       gpio drive <group> <value>
       gpio pwm-bal/pwm-ms
       gpio pwmr <range>
       gpio pwmc <divider>
       gpio load spi / i2c
       gpio gbr <channel>
       gpio gbw <channel> <value>
```

There are many options and functions within this utility. I'll just demonstrate some quick examples of the most useful ones. Once installed, the full details of the utility can be found by this command:

```
$ man 1 gpio
```

Displaying GPIO Settings

The following command can be used to display your GPIO settings:

```
$ gpio readall
+----------+--------+---------+-------+-------+
| wiringPi |  GPIO  |  Name   | Mode  | Value|
+----------+--------+---------+-------+-------+
|    0     |   17   | GPIO 0  |  IN   | High |
|    1     |   18   | GPIO 1  |  IN   | Low  |
|    2     |   27   | GPIO 2  |  OUT  | Low  |
|    3     |   22   | GPIO 3  |  IN   | Low  |
|    4     |   23   | GPIO 4  |  IN   | Low  |
|    5     |   24   | GPIO 5  |  IN   | Low  |
|    6     |   25   | GPIO 6  |  IN   | Low  |
|    7     |    4   | GPIO 7  |  IN   | Low  |
|    8     |    2   | SDA     | ALTo  | High |
|    9     |    3   | SCL     | ALTo  | High |
|   10     |    8   | CEo     |  IN   | Low  |
|   11     |    7   | CE1     |  IN   | Low  |
|   12     |   10   | MOSI    |  IN   | Low  |
|   13     |    9   | MISO    |  IN   | Low  |
|   14     |   11   | SCLK    |  IN   | Low  |
|   15     |   14   | TxD     | ALTo  | High |
|   16     |   15   | RxD     | ALTo  | High |
|   17     |   28   | GPIO8   |  IN   | Low  |
|   18     |   29   | GPIO9   |  IN   | Low  |
|   19     |   30   | GPIO10  |  IN   | Low  |
|   20     |   31   | GPIO11  |  IN   | Low  |
+----------+--------+---------+-------+-------+
```

Reading GPIO

As a convenience, the gpio command allows you to read values from the command line:

```
$ gpio export 27 in
$ gpio -g read 27
0
$ gpio unexportall
```

Use the -g option to specify that the pin number is a GPIO pin number. (I found the need for the -g option irksome.)

Writing GPIO

Like the read function, the gpio command can write values:

```
$ gpio export 27 out
$ gpio -g write 27 1
$ gpio -g read 27
1
$ gpio -g write 27 0
$ gpio -g read 27
0
$ gpio unexportall
```

Use the -g option to specify GPIO pin numbers for the read/write commands.

Modify Drive Levels

The gpio command also enables you to alter the drive levels of the three available pads. The following changes pad 1 to drive level 6 (from 7):

```
$ gpio drive 1 6
```

Use the pads program shown earlier in this chapter to verify the current settings:

```
$ gpio drive 1 6
$ ./pads
07E1002C : 0000001B 1 1 3
07E10030 : 0000001E 1 1 6
07E10034 : 0000001B 1 1 3
```

This kind of change should not be made lightly. If you don't have a sound reason to change these drive levels, it is recommended that you don't.

■ ■ ■

## CHAPTER 11

1-Wire Driver

The 1-Wire protocol was developed by Dallas Semiconductor Corp. initially for the iButton.[37] This communication protocol was attractive enough to be applied to other devices and soon adopted by other manufacturers. This chapter provides an overview of the 1-Wire protocol and how it is supported in the Raspberry Pi.

1-Wire Line and Power

The 1-Wire protocol actually uses two wires:

- *Data*: The single wire used for data communication

- *Ground*: The ground or "return" wire

The 1-Wire protocol was designed for communication with low–data content devices like temperature sensors. It provides for low-cost remote sensing by supplying power over the same wire used for data communications. Each sensor can accept power from the data line while the data line is in the high state (which is also the line's idle state). The small amount of power that is siphoned off charges the chip's internal capacitor (usually about 800 pF).[37]

When the data line is active (going low), the sensor chips continue to run off of their internal capacitors (in parasitic mode). Data communications cause the data line to fluctuate between low and high. So whenever the line level returns high again, even for an instant, the capacitor recharges.

The device also provides an optional V_{DD} pin, allowing power to be supplied to it directly. This is sometimes used when parasitic mode doesn't work well enough. This, of course, requires an added wire, which adds to the cost of the circuit. We'll be focusing on the parasitic mode in this chapter. In parasitic mode, V_{DD} is connected to the ground.

Line Driving

The data line is driven by *open collector* transistors in the master and slave devices. The line is held high by a *pull-up* resistor when the driver transistors are all in the Off state. To initiate a signal, one transistor turns on and thus pulls the line down to ground potential.

Figure 11-1 shows a simplified schematic of the master attached to the bus. Some voltage V (typically, +5 V) is applied to the 1-Wire bus through the pull-up resistor R_{pullup}. When the transistor M_2 is in the Off state, the voltage on the bus remains high because of the pull-up resistor. However, when the master device activates transistor M_2, current is caused to flow from the bus to the ground, acting like a signal short-circuit. Slave devices attached to the bus will see a voltage near zero.

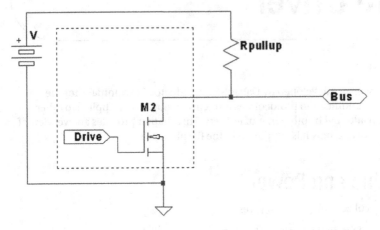

Figure 11-1. *1-Wire driver circuit*

■ **Note**   The Raspbian Linux 1-Wire bus uses GPIO 4 (GPCLK0) pin P1-07.

Likewise, when a slave is signaled to respond, the master listens to the bus while the slave activates its driving transistor. Whenever all driving transistors are off, the bus returns to the high idle state.

The master can request that all slave devices reset. After the master has made this request known, it relinquishes the bus and allows it to return to the high state. All slave devices that are connected to the bus respond by bringing the line low after a short pause. Multiple slaves will bring the line low at the same time, but this is permitted. This informs the master that at least one slave device is attached to the bus. Additionally, this procedure puts all slaves into a known reset state.

Master and Slave

The master device is always in control of the 1-Wire bus. Slaves speak only to the master, and only when requested. There is never slave-to-slave device communication.

If the master finds that communication becomes difficult for some reason, it may force a bus reset. This corrects for an errant slave device that might be jabbering on the line.

Protocol

This section presents a simplistic introduction to the 1-Wire communication protocol. Knowing something about how the signaling works is not only interesting, but may be helpful for troubleshooting. More information is available on the Internet.[38]

Reset

Figure 11-2 provides a simplified timing diagram of the reset procedure for the 1-Wire protocol. When the master driver begins, it must reset the 1-Wire bus to put all the slave devices into a known state.

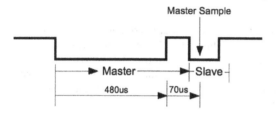

Figure 11-2. 1-Wire reset protocol

For reset, the bus is brought low and held there for approximately 480 μsec. Then the bus is released, and the pull-up resistor brings it high again. After a short time, slave devices connected to the bus start responding by bringing the line low and holding it for a time. Several slaves can participate in this at the same time. The master samples the bus at around 70 μsec after it releases the bus. If it finds the line low, it knows that there is at least one slave connected and responding.

Soon after the master sampling point, all slaves release the bus again and go into a listening state. They do not respond again until the master specifically addresses a slave device. For simplicity, we'll omit the discovery protocol used.

■ **Note** Each slave has a guaranteed unique address.

Data I/O

The data protocol is shown in Figure 11-3. Whether writing a 0 or 1 bit, the sending device brings the bus line low. This announces the start of a data bit.

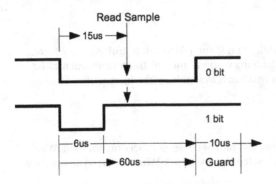

Figure 11-3. 1-Wire read/write of 1 data bit

When a 0 is being transmitted, the line is held low for approximately 60 μsec. Then the bus is released and allowed to return high. When a 1 bit is being transmitted, the line is held low for only about 6 μsec before releasing the bus. Another data bit is not begun until 70 μsec after the start of the previous bit. This leaves a guard time of 10 μsec between bits. The receiver then has ample time to process the bit and gains some signal noise immunity.

The receiver notices a data bit is coming when the line drops low. It then starts a timer and samples the bus at approximately 15 μsec. If the bus is still in the low state, a 0 data bit is registered. Otherwise, the data bit is interpreted as a 1. Having registered a data bit, the receiver then waits further until the line returns high (in the case of a 0 bit). The receiver remains idle until it notices the line going low again, announcing the start of the next bit.

The sender can be either the master or the slave, but the master always has control. Slaves do not write data to the bus unless the master has specifically requested it.

Slave Support

Table 11-1 lists the slave devices that are supported by Raspbian Linux. The module names listed are found in the kernel source directory arch/arm/machbcm2708/slave.

Table 11-1. *1-Wire Slave Driver Support*

Device	Module	Description
DS18S20	w1_therm.c	Precision digital thermometer
DS18B20		Programmable resolution thermometer
DS1822		Econo digital thermometer
DS28EA00		9- to 12-bit digital thermometer with PIO
bq27000	w1_bq27000.c	Highly accurate battery monitor
DS2408	w1_ds2408.c	Eight-channel addressable switch
DS2423	w1_ds2423.c	4 KB RAM with counter
DS2431	w1_ds2431.c	1 KB EEPROM
DS2433	w1_ds2433.c	4 KB EEPROM
DS2760	w1_ds2760.c	Precision Li+ battery monitor
DS2780	w1_ds2780.c	Stand-alone fuel gauge

Reading Temperature

The support for the usual temperature sensors is found in the kernel module w1_therm. When you first boot your Raspbian Linux, that module may not be loaded. You can check for it with the lsmod command:

```
$ lsmod
Module          Size    Used by
snd_bcm2835     12808   1
snd_pcm         74834   1 snd_bcm2835
snd_seq         52536   0
snd_timer       19698   2 snd_seq, snd_pcm
snd_seq_device  6300    1 snd_seq
snd             52489   7 snd_seq_device , snd_timer ,
                        snd_seq , snd_pcm, snd_bcm2835
snd_page_alloc  4951    1 snd_pcm
```

The module w1_therm is not loaded according to the example. This module also depends on the driver module wire. Another thing you can check is the pseudo file system:

```
$ ls -l /sys/bus/w1
ls: cannot access /sys/bus/w1 : No such file or directory
```

169

Having not found the pathname /sys/bus/w1, we have confirmation that the device driver is not loaded.

Loading module w1_therm will bring in most of its module dependents:

```
$ sudo modprobe w1_therm
$ lsmod
Module          Size    Used by
w1_therm        2705    0
wire            23530   1 w1_therm
cn              4649    1 wire
snd_bcm2835     12808   1
snd_pcm         74834   1 snd_bcm2835
...
```

After the wire module is loaded, you'll see the /sys/bus/w1/devices directory. One more module is needed:

```
$ sudo modprobe w1_gpio
$ lsmod
Module          Size    Used by
w1_gpio         1283    0
w1_therm        2705    0
wire            23530   2 w1_therm,w1_gpio
cn              4649    1 wire
snd_bcm2835     12808   1
...
$ cd /sys/bus/w1/devices
$ ls
w1_bus_master1
```

Once module w1_gpio is loaded, there is a bus master driver for GPIO pin 4 (the default GPIO for the 1-Wire bus) at the ready. The bus master makes its presence known by creating directory w1_bus_master1. Change to that directory and list it to see the associated pseudo files within it. Table 11-2 lists the initial set of pseudo files and symlinks found there.

Table 11-2. w1_bus_masterX Files

File	Type	Read Content
driver	Symlink	
power	Directory	
subsystem	Symlink	
uevent	File	DRIVER=w1_master_driver
w1_master_add	File	Write device ID xx-xxxxxxxxxxxx to add slave
w1_master_attempts	File	88
w1_master_max_slave_count	File	10
_master_name	File	w1_bus_master1
w1_master_pointer	File	0xd7032148
w1_master_pullup	File	1
w1_master_remove	File	Write device ID xx-xxxxxxxxxxxx to remove slave
w1_master_search	File	–1
w1_master_slave_count	File	0
w1_master_slaves	File	Not found
w1_master_timeout	File	10

Bus Master

The bus master driver scans for new slave devices every 10 seconds (according to w1_master_timeout). File w1_master_attempts indicates how many scans have been performed to date. File w1_master_slave_count shows how many slaves have been detected out of a maximum of w1_master_max_slave_count. Reading w1_master_slaves provides a list of slaves found or not found.

The following is an example output session produced while two DS18B20 temperature sensors were connected to the bus:

```
$ cd /sys/bus/w1/devices/w1_bus_master1
$ cat w1_master_slaves
28-00000478d75e
28-0000047931b5
$
```

Slave Devices

Figure 11-4 shows the pinout of the Dallas DS18B20 slave device. This temperature sensor is typical of many 1-wire slave devices.

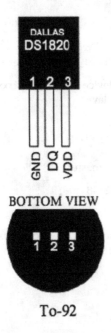

PIN DESCRIPTION

GND - Ground
DQ   - Data In/Out
V_{DD} - Power Supply Voltage

Figure 11-4. DS18B20 pin-out

Slave devices are identified by a pair of digits representing the product family, followed by a hyphen and serial number in hexadecimal. The ID 28-00000478d75e is an example. You might also want to try different devices, like the similar DS18S20. Figure 11-5 illustrates the DS18B20 attached to the Raspberry Pi.

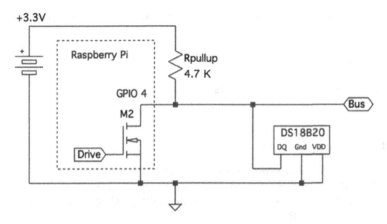

Figure 11-5. *1-Wire with DS18B20 slave circuit*

When things are working correctly, the bus master detects slave devices automatically as part of its periodic scan. If the device you've attached is not showing up within 10 seconds or so, you may want to try forcing it. You can force adding a slave device entry as follows:

```
# cd /sys/bus/w1/devices/w1_bus_master1
# echo 28-0000028f6667 >w1_master_add
```

Upon doing this, subdirectory 28-0000028f6667 will appear, at least until the driver gives up trying to communicate with it (the following line with the ellipsis is abbreviated):

```
# ls -ltr  ./28-0000028f6667
total 0
-rw-r--r--  1  root  root  4096  Jan  30  18:56  uevent
lrwxrwxrwx  1  root  root     0  Jan  30  18:56  subsystem -> ../../../
                                                 bus/w1
-r--r--r--  1  root  root  4096  Jan  30  18:56  w1_slave
Drwxr-xr-x  2  root  root     0  Jan  30  18:56  powerr
-r--r--r--  1  root  root  4096  Jan  30  18:56  name
-r--r--r--  1  root  root  4096  Jan  30  18:56  id
lrwxrwxrwx  1  root  root     0  Jan  30  18:56  driver -> .../w1_
                                                 slave_driver
```

If you want to remove a slave device, you can use the w1_master_remove file. The device will reappear in 10 seconds or so (due to a scanning period), if the device is still physically connected to the bus.

```
# echo  28-0000028f6667 >w1_master_remove
```

The following example shows how two DS18B20 temperature sensors show up on the 1-Wire bus:

```
$ cd /sys/bus/w1/devices
$ ls
28-00000478d75e 28-0000047931b5 w1_bus_master1
$
```

Reading the Temperature

The slave device's temperature can be read by reading its w1_slave pseudo file. In this example, we read two DS18B20 temperature sensors that are supposed to be accurate to ±0.5 °C. Reading these two sensors together should show fairly good agreement (they were in close proximity of each other):

```
$ cat 28-00000478d75e/w1_slave 28-0000047931b5/w1_slave
14 01 4b 46 7f ff 0c 10 b4 : crc=b4 YES
14 01 4b 46 7f ff 0c 10 b4 t=17250
14 01 4b 46 7f ff 0c 10 b4 : crc=b4 YES
14 01 4b 46 7f ff 0c 10 b4 t=17250
$
```

Each sensor brings back two lines of data from the device driver. We see that both sensors agree exactly—that the temperature is 17.250°C. This speaks well for their accuracy. The DS18B20 device also supports a wide temperature range (–55°C to +125°C), which make them good as outdoor sensors.

If the read hangs at this point, it may be that the sensor hasn't fully registered yet. This can happen if you forced adding it, but the driver was unable to communicate with it.

1-Wire GPIO Pin

Raspbian Linux has its driver support for the 1-Wire bus on GPIO 4 (P1-07). This pin is hard-coded in the kernel driver. If you want to change this, look for the definition of W1_GPIO in the source file:

```
arch/arm/mach-bcm2708/bcm2708.c
```

Change the definition of W1_GPIO to the pin you require (found near line 73):

```
// use GPIO 4 for the one-wire GPIO pin, if enabled
#define W1_GPIO 4
```

Then, of course, you'll need to rebuild and install the new kernel.

■ ■ ■

## CHAPTER 12

I2C Bus

The I2C bus, also known as the two-wire interface (TWI), was developed by Philips circa 1982 to allow communication with lower-speed peripherals.[49] It was also economical because it required only two wires (excluding ground and power connections). Since then, other standards have been devised, building upon this framework, such as the SMBus. However, the original I2C bus remains popular as a simple, cost-effective way to connect peripherals.

I2C Overview

Figure 12-1 shows the I2C bus in the Raspberry Pi context. The Raspberry Pi provides the I2C bus using the BCM2835 as the bus master. Notice that the Pi also provides the external pull-up resistors R_1 and R_2, shown inside the dotted lines.

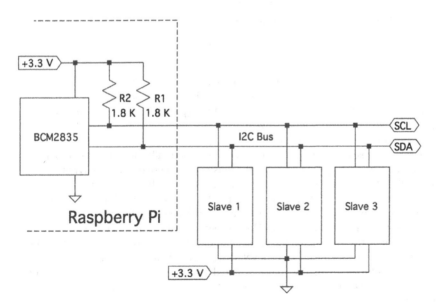

Figure 12-1. *The I2C bus*

The two I2C bus lines are provided on the header strip P1:

	Rev	1.0		Rev	2.0 +	
P1	**GPIO**	**I2C**	**Bus**	**GPIO**	**I2C**	**Bus**
P1-03	0	SDA0	I2C-0	2	SDA1	I2C-1
P1-05	1	SCL0		3	SCL1	

Note that the original Raspberry Pi provided I2C bus 0, but switched to using bus 1 with Rev 2.0 and later units.

The design of the I2C bus is such that multiple peripherals are attached to the SDA and the SCL lines. Each slave (peripheral) has its own unique 7-bit address. For example, the MCP23017 GPIO extender peripheral might be configured with the address of 0x20. Each peripheral is called upon by the master by using this address. All nonaddressed peripherals are expected to remain quiet so that communication can proceed with the selected slave device.

SDA and SCL

The two bus lines used for I2C are as follows:

Line	P1	Idle	Description
SDA	P1-03	High	Serial data line
SCL	P1-05	High	Serial clock line

Both masters and slaves take turns at "grabbing the bus" at various times. Master and slave use open-drain transistors to drive the bus. It is because all participants are using open-drain drivers that pull-up resistors must be used (provided by the Pi). Otherwise, the data and clock lines would float between handoffs.

The open-drain driver design allows all participants to drive the bus lines—just not at the same time. Slaves, for example, turn off their line drivers, allowing the master to drive the signal lines. The slaves just listen, until the master calls them by address. When the slave is required to answer, the slave will then assert its driver, thus grabbing the line. It is assumed by the slave that the master has already released the bus at this point. When the slave completes its own transmission, it releases the bus, allowing the master to resume.

The idle state for both lines is high. The high state for the Raspberry Pi is +3.3 V. Other systems may use +5 V signaling. When shopping for I2C peripherals, you'll want to choose ones that will operate at the 3 V level. Otherwise, 5 V peripherals can sometimes be used with careful planning or with use of signal adapters. The DS1307 Real-Time clock project is one such a case that is covered in Chapter 4 of *Experimenting with Raspberry Pi* (Apress, 2014).

Multimaster and Arbitration

The I2C protocol does support the idea of multiple masters. This complicates things, because two masters may grab the bus and transmit at the same time. When this happens, a process of arbitration is used to resolve the clash.

Each transmitting master simultaneously monitors what it sees on the bus that it is driving. If a discrepancy is seen between what it is transmitting and what it is sensing on the bus line, it knows that it must release the bus and cease. The first node to notice conflict is required to release the bus. The other that has not noticed any discrepancy is free to continue its transmission, since its message has not been affected. If it too sees a problem, it will also cease and retry later.

Not all devices support this arbitration. Ones that do are usually advertised as having *multimaster support*. Multimaster arbitration is not covered in this book, since this is an advanced I2C topic.

Bus Signaling

The start and stop bits are special in the I2C protocol. The start bit is illustrated in Figure 12-2. Notice the SDA line transition from high to low, while the clock remains in the high (idle) state. The clock will follow by going low after 1/2 bit time following the SDA transition. This special signal combination informs all connected devices to "listen up," since the next piece of information transmitted will be the device address.

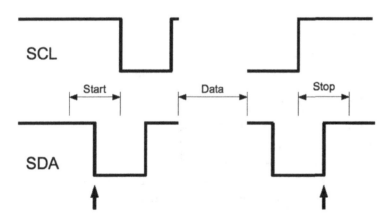

Figure 12-2. *I2C start/stop signaling*

The stop bit is also special in that it allows slave devices to know whether more information is coming. When the SDA line transitions from low to high midway through a bit cell, it is interpreted as a *stop bit*. The stop bit signals the end of the message.

There is also the concept of a *repeated start*, often labeled in diagrams as *SR*. This signal is electrically identical to the start bit, except that it occurs within a message in place of a stop bit. This signals to the peripheral that more data is being sent or required as part of another message.

Data Bits

Data bit timings are approximately as shown in Figure 12-3. The SDA line is expected to stabilize high or low according to the data bit being sent, prior to the SCL line going high. The receiver clocks in the data on the falling edge of SCL, and the process repeats for the next data bit. Note that most significant bits are transmitted first.

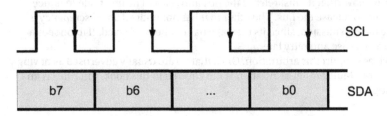

Figure 12-3. I2C Data bit transmission

Message Formats

Figure 12-4 displays two example I2C messages that can be used with the MCP23017 chip (covered in Chapter 2 of *Experimenting with Raspberry Pi* [Apress, 2014]). The simplest message is the write register request.

MCP23017 Write Register Message:

S	A6	A5	...	A1	A0	W	A	R7	R6	...	R2	R1	R0	A	D7	D6	...	D2	D1	D0	A	P
	Addr + Write							Register Number							Data							

MCP23017 Read Register Message:

S	A6	A5	...	A1	A0	W	A	R7	R6	...	R2	R1	R0	A
	Addr + Write							Register Number						

S	Start
P	Stop
A	ACK/NAK
SR	Start, Repeated

SR	A6	A5	...	A1	A0	R	A	D7	D6	...	D2	D1	D0	A	P
	Addr + Read							Data							

Figure 12-4. Example I2C messages

The diagram shows each message starting with the S (start) bit and ending with a P (stop) bit. After the start bit, each message begins with a byte containing the 7-bit peripheral address and a read/write bit. Every peripheral must read this byte in order to determine whether the message is addressed to it.

The addressed peripheral is expected to return an ACK/NAK bit after the address is sent. If the peripheral fails to respond for any reason, the line will go high due to the pull-up resistor, indicating a NAK. The master, upon seeing a NAK, will send a stop bit and terminate the transmission.

When the peripheral ACKs the address byte, the master then continues to write when the request is a write. The first example shows the MCP23017 8-bit register number being written next. This indicates which of the peripheral's registers is to be written to. The peripheral will then ACK the register number, allowing the master to follow with the data byte to be written into the selected register. This too must be ACKed. If the master has no more data to send, the P (stop) bit is sent to end the transmission. Otherwise, more data bytes could follow with the sequence ending with the stop bit.

The second example in Figure 12-4 shows how a message may be composed of both write and read messages. The initial sequence looks like the write, but this only writes a register number into the peripheral. Once the register number is ACKed, the master then sends an SR (start, repeated) bit. This tells the peripheral that no more write data is coming and to expect a peripheral address next. Since the address transmitted specifies the same peripheral, the same peripheral responds with an ACK. This request is a read, so the peripheral continues to respond with 8 bits of the requested read data, with the master ACKing the data received. The master terminates the message with a P (stop) to indicate that no more data is to be read.

Many peripherals will support an *auto-increment* register mode. This is a feature of the peripheral, however, and not all devices support this. Once a peripheral's register has been established by a write, successive reads or writes can occur in auto-increment mode, with the register being incremented with each byte transferred. This results in more-efficient transfers.

Which I2C Bus?

Before we look at the I2C software API provided by Raspbian Linux, you should first determine which I2C bus you'll be working with. Early Raspberry Pi revisions provided I2C bus 0 on header strip P1, while later units changed this to bus 1. This will matter to both commands and programs communicating with I2C peripherals.

The "Identification" section of Chapter 5 discusses how to identify your Pi by displaying the firmware code from /proc/cpuinfo. What is displayed as a Revision is actually more of a firmware code. The following is a quick check example:

```
$ grep Revision /proc/cpuinfo
Revision        : 000f
```

From this information, use the firmware code (revision) number to determine which I2C bus to use:

		SDA	SCL
Revision	I2C Bus	P1-03	P1-05
0002	0	GPIO-0	GPIO-1
0003	0		
0004+	1	GPIO-2	GPIO-3

I2C Bus Speed

Unlike the SPI bus, the I2C bus operates at a fixed speed within Raspbian Linux. The SoC document claims I2C operation up to 400 kHz, but the reported clock rate during the Raspbian Linux boot is 100 kHz:

```
$ dmesg | grep -i i2c
[1005.08] i2c /dev entries driver
[1026.43] bcm2708_i2c bcm2708_i2c.0: BSC0 Controller at. . . (baudrate 100k)
[1026.43] bcm2708_i2c bcm2708_i2c.1: BSC1 Controller at. . . (baudrate 100k)
```

Don't be alarmed if the preceding grep command doesn't provide any output. Later versions of Raspbian didn't load bcm2708_i2c at boot time. You should see the same messages in the /var/log/syslog after you manually load the module as shown here:

```
$ sudo modprobe i2c_bcm2708
$ tail /var/log/syslog
. . .
Mar 12 20:16:55 raspberrypi kernel: [168.845802] bcm2708_i2c bcm2708_i2c.0: \
  BSC0 Controller at 0x20205000 (irq 79) (baudrate 100k)
Mar 12 20:16:55 raspberrypi kernel: [168.846423] bcm2708_i2c bcm2708_i2c.1: \
  BSC1 Controller at 0   x20804000 (irq 79) (baudrate 100k)
```

Tools

Working with I2C peripherals is made easier with the use of utilities. These I2C utilities are easily installed using the following command:

```
$ sudo apt-get install i2c-tools
```

The i2c-tools package includes the following utilities:

i2cdetect: Detects peripherals on the I2C line

i2cdump: Dumps values from an I2C peripheral

i2cset: Sets I2C registers and values

i2cget: Gets I2C registers and values

Each of these utilities has a man page available for additional information. We'll be using some of these commands in this chapter and in later parts of this book.

I2C API

In this section, we'll look at the bare-metal C language API for the I2C bus transactions. An application using this API is provided in Chapter 2 of *Experimenting with Raspberry Pi* (Apress, 2014).

Kernel Module Support

Access to the I2C bus is provided through the use of kernel modules. If lsmod indicates that the drivers are not loaded, you can load them at the command line:

```
$ sudo modprobe i2c-dev
$ sudo modprobe i2c-bcm2708
```

Once these modules are loaded, i2cdetect should be able to see bus-level support. On Revision 2.0 and later Raspberry Pis, the i2c-0 bus is for internal use. The user bus is shown as i2c-1. On early Pis this is reversed.

```
$ i2cdetect -l
i2c-0   unknown        bcm2708_i2c.0          N/A
i2c-1   unknown        bcm2708_i2c.1          N/A
```

After the driver support is available, the device nodes should appear under /dev:

```
$ ls -l /dev/i2c*
crw-rw---T 1 root root 89, 0 Feb 18 23:53  /dev/i2c-0
crw-rw---T 1 root root 89, 1 Feb 18 23:53  /dev/i2c-1
```

Header Files

The following header files should be included in an I2C program:

```
#include <sys/ioctl.h>
#include <linux/i2c-dev.h>
```

open(2)

Working with I2C devices is much like working with files. You'll open a file descriptor, do some I/O operations with it, and then close it. The one difference is that you'll want to use ioctl(2) calls instead of the usual read(2)/write(2) calls.

```
#include <sys/types.h>
#include <sys/stat.h>
#include <fcntl.h>

int open(const char *pathname, int flags, mode_t mode);
```

where

> pathname is the name of the file/directory/driver that you need to open/create.

> flags is the list of optional flags (use O_RDWR for reading and writing).

> mode is the permission bits to create a file (omit argument, or supply zero when not creating).

> returns -1 (error code in errno) or open file descriptor >= 0 .

Error	Description
EACCES	Access to the file is not allowed.
EFAULT	The pathname points outside your accessible address space.
EMFILE	The process already has the maximum number of files open.
ENFILE	The system limit on the total number of open files has been reached.
ENOMEM	Insufficient kernel memory was available.

To work with an I2C bus controller, your application must open the driver, made available at the device node:

```
int fd;
```

```
fd = open("/dev/i2c-1",O_RDWR);
if ( fd < 0 ) {
    perror("Opening /dev/i2c-1");
```

Note that the device node (/dev/i2c-1) is owned by root, so you'll need elevated privileges to open it or have your program use setuid(2).

Ioctl(2,I2C_FUNC)

In I2C code, a check is normally performed to make sure that the driver has the right support. The I2C_FUNC ioctl(2) call allows the calling program to query the I2C capabilities. The capability flags returned are documented in Table 12-1.

```
long funcs;
int rc;
```

```
rc = ioctl(fd,I2C_FUNCS,&funcs);
if ( rc < 0 ) {
    perror("ioctl(2,I2C_FUNCS)");
    abort();
}
```

```
/* Check that we have plain I2C support */
assert(funcs & I2C_FUNC_I2C);
```

Table 12-1. *I2C_FUNC bits*

Bit Mask	Description
I2C_FUNC_I2C	Plain I2C is supported (non SMBus)
I2C_FUNC_10BIT_ADDR	Supports 10-bit addresses
I2C_FUNC_PROTOCOL_MANGLING	*Supports:*
	I2C_M_IGNORE_NAK
	I2C_M_REV_DIR_ADDR
	I2C_M_NOSTART
	I2C_M_NO_RD_ACK

The assert() macro used here checks that at least plain I2C support exists. Otherwise, the program aborts.

ioctl(2,I2C_RDWR)

While it is possible to use ioctl(2,I2C_SLAVE) and then use read(2) and write(2) calls, this tends not to be practical. Consequently, the use of the ioctl(2,I2C_RDWR) system call will be promoted here instead. This system call allows considerable flexibility in carrying out complex I2C I/O transactions.

The general API for any ioctl(2) call is as follows:

```
#include <sys/ioctl.h>

int ioctl(int fd, int request, argp);
```

where

> fd is the open file descriptor.
>
> request is the I/O command to perform.
>
> argp is an argument related to the command (type varies according to request).
>
> returns -1 (error code in errno), number of msgs completed (when request = I2C_RDWR).

Error	Description
EBADF	fd is not a valid descriptor.
EFAULT	argp references an inaccessible memory area.
EINVAL	request or argp is not valid.

When the request argument is provided as I2C_RDWR, the argp argument is a pointer to struct i2c_rdwr_ioctl_data. This structure points to a list of messages and indicates how many of them are involved.

```
struct i2c_rdwr_ioctl_data {
    struct i2c_msg  *msgs;    /* ptr to array of simple messages */
    int             nmsgs;    /* number of messages to exchange */
};
```

The individual I/O messages referenced by the preceding structure are described by struct i2c_msg:

```
struct i2c_msg {
    __u16      addr;    /* 7/10 bit slave address */
    __u16      flags;   /* Read/Write & options */
    __u16      len;     /* No. of bytes in buf */
    __u8       *buf;    /* Data buffer */
};
```

The members of this structure are as follows:

addr: Normally this is the 7-bit slave address, unless flag
I2C_M_TEN and function I2C_FUNC_10BIT_ADDR are used. Must
be provided for each message.

flags: Valid flags are listed in Table 12-2. Flag I2C_M_RD
indicates the operation is a read. Otherwise, a write operation
is assumed when this flag is absent.

buf: The I/O buffer to use for reading/writing this message
component.

len: The number of bytes to read/write in this message
component.

Table 12-2. I2C Capability Flags

Flag	Description
I2C_M_TEN	10-bit slave address used
I2C_M_RD	Read into buffer
I2C_M_NOSTART	Suppress (Re)Start bit
I2C_M_REV_DIR_ADDR	Invert R/W bit
I2C_M_IGNORE_NAK	Treat NAK as ACK
I2C_M_NO_RD_ACK	Read will not have ACK
I2C_M_RECV_LEN	Buffer can hold 32 additional bytes

An actual ioctl(2,I2C_RDWR) call would be coded something like the following.
In this example, a MCP23017 *register* address of 0x15 is being written out to peripheral
address 0x20, followed by a read of 1 byte:

```
int fd;
struct i2c_rdwr_ioctl_data msgset;
struct i2c_msg iomsgs[2];
static unsigned char reg_addr[] = {0x15};
unsigned char rbuf[1];
int rc;

iomsgs[0].addr    = 0x20;      /* MCP23017-A */
iomsgs[0].flags  = 0;          /* Write operation. */
iomsgs[0].buf    = reg_addr;
iomsgs[0].len    = 1;
```

```
iomsgs[1].addr   = iomsgs[0].addr;   /* Same MCP23017-A */
iomsgs[1].flags  = I2C_M_RD;         /* Read operation */
iomsgs[1].buf    = rbuf;
iomsgs[1].len    = 1;

msgset.msgs      = iomsgs;
msgset.nmsgs     = 2;

rc = ioctl(fd,I2C_RDWR,&msgset);
if ( rc < 0 ) {
    perror("ioctl (2, I2C_RDWR)");
```

The example shown defines iomsgs[0] as a write of 1 byte, containing a register number. The entry iomsgs[1] describes a read of 1 byte from the peripheral. These two messages are performed in one ioctl(2) transaction. The flags member of iomsgs[x] determines whether the operation is a read (I2C_M_RD) or a write (0).

■ **Note** Don't confuse the peripheral's internal register with the peripheral's I2C address.

Each of the iomsgs[x].addr members must contain a valid I2C peripheral address. Each message can potentially address a different peripheral, though there are no examples of this in this book. The ioctl(2) will return an error with the first message failure. For this reason, you may not always want to combine multiple messages in one ioctl(2) call, especially when different devices are involved.

The returned value, when successful, is the number of struct i2c_msg messages successfully performed.

## CHAPTER 13

SPI Bus

The Serial Peripheral Interface bus, known affectionately as *spy*, is a synchronous serial interface that was named by Motorola.[39] The SPI protocol operates in full-duplex mode, allowing it to send and receive data simultaneously. Generally speaking, SPI has a speed advantage over the I2C protocol but requires more connections.

SPI Basics

Devices on the SPI bus communicate on a master/slave basis. Multiple slaves coexist on a given SPI bus, with each slave being selected for communication by a slave select signal (also known as chip select). Figure 13-1 shows the Raspberry Pi as the master communicating with a slave. Additional slaves would be connected as shown with the exception that a different slave select signal would be used.

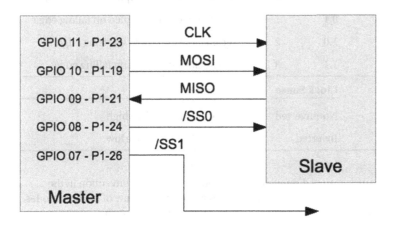

Figure 13-1. SPI interface

Data is transmitted from the master to the slave by using the MOSI line (master out, slave in). As each bit is being sent out by the master, the slave sends data bits on the MISO line (master in, slave out). Bits are shifted out of the master and into the slave. Simultaneously, bits are shifted out of the slave and into the master. Both transfers occur to the beat of the system clock (CLK).

187

Many SPI devices support only 8-bit transfers, while others are more flexible. The SPI bus is a de facto standard, meaning that there is no standard for data transfer width and SPI mode.[39] The SPI controller can also be configured to transmit the most significant or the least significant bit first. All of this flexibility can result in confusion.

SPI Mode

SPI operates in one of four possible clock signaling modes, based on two parameters:

Parameter	Description
CPOL	Clock polarity
CPHA	Clock phase

Each parameter has two possibilities, resulting in four possible SPI modes of operation. Table 13-1 lists all four modes available. Note that a given mode is often referred to by using a pair of numbers like 1,0 or simply as mode 2 (for the same mode, as shown in the table). Both types of references are shown in the Mode column.

Table 13-1. SPI Modes

CPOL	CPHA	Mode		Description
0	0	0,0	0	Noninverted clock, sampled on rising edge
0	1	0,1	1	Noninverted clock, sampled on falling edge
1	0	1,0	2	Inverted clock, sampled on rising edge
1	1	1,1	3	Inverted clock, sampled on falling edge
		Clock Sense		**Description**
		Noninverted		Signal is idle low, active high
		Inverted		Signal is idle high, active low

Peripheral manufacturers did not define a standard signaling convention in the beginning, so SPI controllers allow configuration to accommodate any of the four modes. However, once a mode has been chosen, all slaves on the same bus must agree.

Signaling

The clock polarity determines the idle clock level, while the phase determines whether the data line is sampled on the rising or falling clock signal. Figure 13-2 shows mode 0,0, which is perhaps the preferred form of SPI signaling. In Figure 13-2, the slave is selected first, by bringing the $\overline{SS}$ (slave select) active. Only one slave can be selected at a time, since there must be only one slave driving the MISO line. Shortly after the slave is selected, the master drives the MOSI line, and the slave simultaneously drives the MISO line with the first data bit. This can be the most or least significant bit, depending on how the controller is configured. The diagram shows the least significant bit first.

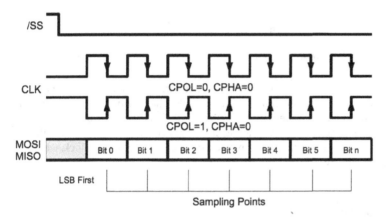

Figure 13-2. SPI signaling, modes 0 and 2

In mode 0,0 the first bit is clocked into the master and slave when the clock line falls from high to low. This clock transition is positioned midway in the data bit cell. The remaining bits are successively clocked into master and slave simultaneously as the clock transitions from high to low. The transmission ends when the master deactivates the slave select line. When the clock polarity is reversed (CPOL = 1, CPHA = 0), the clock signal shown in Figure 13-2 is simply inverted. The data is clocked at the same time in the data cell, but on the rising edge of the clock instead.

Figure 13-3 shows the clock signals with the phase set to 1 (CPHA = 1). When the clock is noninverted (CPOL = 0), the data is clocked on the rising edge. Note that the clock must transition to its nonidle state one-half clock cycle earlier than when the phase is 0 (CPHA = 0). When the SPI mode is 1,1, the data is clocked in on the falling edge of the clock.

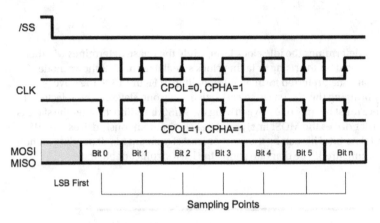

Figure 13-3. *SPI signaling modes 1 and 3*

While the four different modes can be confusing, it is important to realize that the data is sampled at the same times within the data bit cells. The data bit is always sampled at the midpoint of the data cell. When the clock phase is 0 (CPHA = 0), the data is sampled on the trailing edge of the clock, whether falling or rising according to CPOL. When the clock phase is 1 (CPHA = 1), the data is sampled on the leading edge of the clock, whether rising or falling according to CPOL.

Slave Selection

While some protocols address their slaves by using transmitted data, the SPI bus simply uses a dedicated line for each slave. The Raspberry Pi dedicates the GPIO pins listed in Table 13-2 as slave select lines (also known as chip enable lines).

Table 13-2. *Raspberry Pi Built-in Chip Enable Pins*

GPIO	Chip Enable	P1
8	$\overline{CE0}$	P1-24
7	$\overline{CE1}$	P1-26

The Raspbian Linux kernel driver supports the use of only these two chip enable lines. However, the driver is designed such that you don't have to use them, or only these. It is possible, for example, to add a third GPIO pin as a slave select. The application simply takes responsibility for activating the slave select GPIO line prior to the data I/O and deactivates it after. When the driver is controlling the two slave selects, this is done automatically.

Driver Support

Raspbian Linux supports SPI through the spi_bcm2708 kernel module. As a loadable kernel module, it may not be loaded by default. Check for it by using the lsmod command:

```
$ lsmod
Module            Size    Used by
spidev            5136    0
spi_bcm2708       4401    0
...
```

If you would like the module loaded by default after a reboot, edit the /etc/modprobe.d file raspi-blacklist.conf. In the file, look for the line

```
blacklist spi-bcm2708
```

and change that to a comment line, by putting a # character in front, as follows:

```
# blacklist spi-bcm2708
```

With that module un-blacklisted, the module will automatically be loaded with each new reboot.

The kernel module can be manually loaded by using modprobe command:

```
$ sudo modprobe spi_bcm2708
```

This loads the module and its dependents. Once the kernel module support is present, the device driver nodes should appear:

```
$ ls /dev/spi*
/dev/spidev0.0  /dev/spidev0.1
$
```

These two device nodes are named according to which slave select should be activated, as shown in Table 13-3.

Table 13-3. *SPI Device Nodes*

Pathname	Bus	Device	GPIO	$\overline{SS}$
/dev/spidev0.0	0	0	8	$\overline{CE0}$
/dev/spidev0.1	0	1	7	$\overline{CE1}$

If you open either of these device nodes by applying the option SPI_NO_CS, the node chosen makes no difference. Macro SPI_NO_CS indicates that slave select will be performed by the application instead of the driver, if any select is used at all. (When only one slave device is attached, the peripheral can be permanently selected.)

SPI API

The bare-metal API for SPI involves calls to ioctl(2) to configure the interface and further calls to ioctl(2) for simultaneous read and write. The usual read(2) and write(2) system calls can be used, when a one-sided transfer is being performed.

Header Files

The header files needed for SPI programming are as follows:

```
#include <fcntl.h>
#include <unistd.h>
#include <stdint.h>
#include <sys/ioctl.h>
#include <linux/types.h>
#include <linux/spi/spidev.h>
```

The spidev.h include file defines several macros and the struct spi_ioc_transfer. Table 13-4 lists the main macros that are declared. The macros SPI_CPOL and SPI_CPHA are used in the definitions of the values SPI_MODE_x. If you prefer, it is possible to use SPI_CPOL and SPI_CPHA in place of the mode macros.

Table 13-4. *SPI Macro Definitions*

Macro	Supported	Description
SPI_CPOL	Yes	Clock polarity inverted (CPOL = 1)
SPI_CPHA	Yes	Clock phase is 1 (CPHA = 1)
SPI_MODE_0	Yes	SPI Mode 0,0 (CPOL = 0, CPHA = 0)
SPI_MODE_1	Yes	SPI Mode 0,1 (CPOL = 0, CPHA = 1)
SPI_MODE_2	Yes	SPI Mode 1,0 (CPOL = 1, CPHA = 0)
SPI_MODE_3	Yes	SPI Mode 1,1 (CPOL = 1, CPHA = 1)
SPI_CS_HIGH	Yes	Chip select is active high
SPI_LSB_FIRST	No	LSB is transmitted first
SPI_3WIRE	No	Use 3-Wire data I/O mode
SPI_LOOP	No	Loop the MOSI/MISO data line
SPI_NO_CS	Yes	Do not apply Chip Select
SPI_READY	No	Enable extra Ready signal

Communicating with an SPI device consists of the following system calls:

open(2): Opens the SPI device driver node

read(2): Reads with 0 bytes being transmitted

write(2): Writes data while discarding received data

ioctl(2): For configuration and bidirectional I/O

close(2): Closes the SPI device driver node

In SPI communication, the use of read(2) and write(2) is unusual. Normally, ioctl(2) is used to facilitate simultaneous read and write transfers.

Open Device

In order to perform SPI communication through the kernel driver, you need to open one of the device nodes by using open(2). The general format of the device pathname is

```
/dev/spidev<bus>.<device>
```

as we saw earlier. The following is a code snippet opening bus 0, device 0.

```
int fd;

fd = open("/dev/spidev0.0",O_RDWR);
if ( fd < 0 ) {
    perror("Unable to open SPI driver");
    exit(1);
}
```

SPI communication involves both reading and writing, so the driver is opened for read and write (O_RDWR).

SPI Mode Macros

Before SPI communications can be performed, the mode of communication needs to be configured. Table 13-5 lists the C language macros that can be used to configure the SPI mode to be used.

Table 13-5. SPI Mode Macros

Macro	Effect	Comments
SPI_CPOL	CPOL = 1	Or use SPI_MODE_x
SPI_CPHA	CPHA = 1	Or use SPI_MODE_x
SPI_CS_HIGH	SS is active high	Unusual
SPI_NO_CS	Don't assert select	Not used/application controlled

These bit values are simply or-ed together to specify the options that are required. The use of SPI_CPOL implies CPOL = 1. Its absence implies CPOL = 0. Similarly, the use of SPI_CPHA implies CPHA = 1 (otherwise, CPHA = 0). The options SPI_MODE_x use the SPI_CPOL and SPI_CPHA macros to define them. You don't need to use them both in your code. The mode definitions are shown here:

```
#define SPI_MODE_0 (0|0)
#define SPI_MODE_1 (0|SPI_CPHA)
#define SPI_MODE_2 (SPI_CPOL|0)
#define SPI_MODE_3 (SPI_CPOL|SPI_CPHA)
```

The unsupported options are not shown, though one or more of these could be supported in the future.

■ **Note** The mode values SPI_LOOP, SPI_LSB_FIRST, SPI_3WIRE, and SPI_READY are not currently supported in the wheezy release of Raspbian Linux.

The following is an example that defines SPI_MODE_0:

```
uint8_t mode = SPI_MODE_0;
int rc;

rc = ioctl(fd,SPI_IOC_WR_MODE,&mode);
if ( rc < 0 ) {
    perror("Can't set SPI write mode.");
```

If you'd like to find out how the SPI driver is currently configured, you can read the SPI mode with ioctl(2) as follows:

```
uint8_t mode;
int rc;

rc = ioctl(fd,SPI_IOC_RD_MODE,&mode);
if ( rc < 0 ) {
    perror("Can't get SPI read mode.");
```

Bits per Word

The SPI driver also needs to know how many bits per I/O word are to be transmitted. While the driver will likely default to 8 bits, it is best not to depend on that. This can be configured with the following ioctl(2) call:

```
uint8_t bits = 8;
int rc;

rc = ioctl(fd, SPI_IOC_WR_BITS_PER_WORD,&bits);
if ( rc < 0 ) {
    perror ("Can't set bits per SPI word.");
```

■ **Note** The SPI driver in the Raspbian wheezy release supports only 8-bit transfers.

The currently configured value can be fetched with ioctl(2) as follows:

```
uint8_t bits;
int rc;

rc = ioctl(fd,SPI_IOC_RD_BITS_PER_WORD,&bits);
if ( rc == -1 ) {
    perror("Can't get bits per SPI word.");
```

When the number of bits is not an even multiple of eight, the bits are assumed to be right-justified. For example, if the word length is set to 4 bits, the least significant 4 bits are transmitted. The higher-order bits are ignored.

Likewise, when receiving data, the least significant bits contain the data. All of this is academic on the Pi, however, since the driver supports only byte-wide transfers.

Clock Rate

To configure the data transmission rate, you can set the clock rate with ioctl(2) as follows:

```
uint32_t speed = 500000; /* Hz */
int rc;

rc = ioctl(fd,SPI_IOC_WR_MAX_SPEED_HZ,&speed);
if ( rc < 0 ) {
    perror("Can't configure SPI clock rate.");
```

The current configured clock rate can be fetched by using the following ioctl(2) call:

```
uint32_t speed; /* Hz */
int rc;

rc = ioctl(fd,SPI_IOC_RD_MAX_SPEED_HZ,&speed);
if ( rc < 0 ) {
    perror("Can't get SPI clock rate.");
```

Data I/O

SPI communication involves transmitting data while simultaneously receiving data. For this reason, the read(2) and write(2) system calls are usually inappropriate. The ioctl(2) call can, however, perform a simultaneous read and write.

The SPI_IOC_MESSAGE(n) form of the ioctl(2) call uses the following structure as its argument:

```
struct spi_ioc_transfer {
    __u64    tx_buf;           /* Ptr to tx buffer */
    __u64    rx_buf;           /* Ptr to rx buffer */
    __u32    len;              /* # of bytes */
    __u32    speed_hz;         /* Clock rate in Hz */
    __u16    delay_usecs;      /* Delay in microseconds */
    __u8     bits_per_word;    /* Bits per "word" */
    __u8     cs_change;        /* Apply chip select */
    __u32    pad;              /* Reserved */
};
```

The tx_buf and rx_buf structure members are defined as a 64-bit unsigned integers (__u64). For this reason, you must cast your buffer pointers when making assignments to them:

```
uint8_t tx[32], rx[32];
struct spi_ioc_transfer tr;

tr.tx_buf = (unsigned long) tx;
tr.rx_buf = (unsigned long ) rx;
```

On the Raspberry Pi, you will see example code that simply casts the pointers to unsigned long. The compiler automatically promotes these 32-bit values to a 64-bit value. This is safe on the Pi because the pointer value is a 32-bit value.

If you do not wish to receive data (maybe because it is "don't care" data), you can null out the receive buffer:

```
uint8_t tx[32];
struct spi_ioc_transfer tr;

tr.tx_buf = (unsigned long) tx;
tr.rx_buf = 0;                  /* ignore received data */
```

Note that to receive data, the master must always transmit data to shift data out of the slave peripheral. If any byte transmitted will do, you can omit the transmit buffer. Zero bytes will then be automatically transmitted by the driver to shift the slave data out onto the MISO line.

It is also permissible to transmit from the buffer you're receiving into:

```
uint8_t io[32];
struct spi_ioc_transfer tr;

tr.tx_buf = (unsigned long) io;      /* Transmit buffer */
tr.rx_buf = (unsigned long) io;      /* is also recv buffer */
```

The len structure member indicates the number of bytes for the I/O transfer. Receive and transmit buffers (when both used) are expected to transfer the same number of bytes.

The member speed_hz defines the clock rate that you wish to use for this I/O, in Hz. This overrides any value configured in the mode setup, for the duration of the I/O. The value will be automatically rounded down to a supported clock rate when necessary.

When the value speed_hz is 0, the previously configured clock rate is used (SPI_IOC_WR_MAX_SPEED_HZ).

When the delay_usecs member is nonzero, it specifies the number of microseconds to delay between transfers. It is applied at the end of a transfer, rather than at the start. When there are multiple I/O transfers in a single ioctl(2) request, this allows time in between so that the peripheral can process the data.

The bits_per_word member defines how many bits there are in a "word" unit. Often the unit is 1 byte (8 bits), but it need not be (but note that the Raspbian Linux driver supports only 8 bits).

An application might use 9 bits to transmit the 8-bit byte and a parity bit, for example. The bits communicated on the SPI bus are taken from the least significant bits of the buffer bytes. This is true even when transmitting the most significant bit first.

When the bits_per_word value is 0, the previously configured value from SPI_IOC_WR_BITS_PER_WORD is used. (See drivers/spi/spi-bcm2708.c in the function bcm2708_process_transfer()).

▓ **Note** The Raspbian wheezy driver requires that bits_per_word is the value 8 or 0.

The cs_change member is treated as a Boolean value. When 0, no chip select is performed by the driver. The application is expected to do what is necessary to notify the peripheral that it is selected (usually a GPIO pin is brought low). Once the I/O has completed, the application then must normally unselect the slave peripheral.

When the cs_change member is true (non-zero), the slave selected will *depend on the device pathname that was opened*. The bus and the slave address are embedded in the device name:

```
/dev/spidev<bus>.<device>
```

When cs_change is true, the driver asserts *GPIO8* for spidev0.0 and asserts *GPIO7* for spidev0.1 prior to I/O and then deactivates the same upon completion. Of course, using these two nodes requires two different open(2) calls.

The SPI_IOC_MESSAGE(n) macro is used in the ioctl(2) call to perform one or more SPI I/O operations. The macro is unusual because it requires an argument *n*. (Perhaps someone will take it upon themselves someday to clean this interface up to work like I2C.) This specifies how many I/O transfers you would like to perform. An array of spi_ioc_transfer structures is declared and configured for each transfer required, as shown in the next example:

```
struct spi_ioc_transfer io[3];    /* Define 3 transfers */
int rc;

io[0].tx_buf = . . . ;            /* Configure I/O */
...
io[2].bits_per_word = 8;

rc = ioctl(fd,SPI_IOC_MESSAGE(3),& io[0]);
```

The preceding example will perform three I/O transfers. Since the application never gets to perform any GPIO manipulation between these I/Os, this applies to communicating with one particular slave device.

The following example code brings all of the concepts together, to demonstrate one I/O. The spi_ioc_transfer structure is initialized so that 32 bytes are transmitted and simultaneously 32 are received.

```
uint8_t tx[32], rx[32];
struct spi_ioc_transfer tr;
int rc;

tr.tx_buf        = (unsigned long) tx;
tr.rx_buf        = (unsigned long) rx;
tr.len           = 32;
tr.delay_usecs   = delay;
tr.speed_hz      = speed;
tr.bits_per_word = bits;
```

```
rc = ioctl(fd,SPI_IOC_MESSAGE(1),&tr);
if ( rc < 1 ) {
    perror("Can't send spi message");
```

Here a single I/O transmission occurs, with data being sent from array tx and received into array rx.

The return value from the ioctl(2) call returns the number of bytes transferred (32 in the example). Otherwise, -1 is returned to indicate that an error has occurred.

Close

Like all Unix I/O operations, the device is closed when the open file descriptor is no longer required:

```
close(fd);
```

Write

The write(2) system call can be used, if the received data is unimportant. Note, however, that no delay is applied with this call.

Read

The read(2) system call is actually inappropriate for SPI since the master must transmit data on MOSI in order for the slave to send bits back on the MISO line. However, when read(2) is used, the driver will automatically send out 0 bits as necessary to accomplish the read. (Be careful that your peripheral will accept 0 bytes without unintended consequences.) Like the write(2) call, no delay is provided.

SPI Testing

When developing your SPI communication software, you can perform a simple loopback test to test your framework. Once the framework checks out, you can then turn your attention to communicating with the actual device.

While the Raspbian Linux driver does not support the SPI_LOOP mode bit (in the wheezy release), you can still physically loop your SPI bus by connecting a wire from the MOSI output back to the MISO input pin (connect GPIO 10 to GPIO 9).

A simple program, shown next, demonstrates this type of loopback test. It will write out 4 bytes (0x12, 0x23, 0x45, and 0x67) to the SPI driver. Because you have wired the MOSI pin to the MISO input, anything transmitted will also be received.

When the program executes, it will report the number of bytes received and four hexadecimal values:

```
$ sudo ./spiloop
rc=4 12 23 45 67
$
```

If you remove the wire between MOSI and MISO, and connect the MISO to a high (+3.3 V), you should be able to read 0xFF for all of the received bytes. If you then connect MISO to ground, 0x00 will be received for each byte instead. (Be certain to apply to the correct pin, since applying high or low to an output can damage it, and do not apply +5 V.)

```c
1  /*********************************************************************
2   * spiloop.c - Example loop test
3   * Connect MOSI (GPIO 10) to MISO (GPIO 9)
4   *********************************************************************/
5  #include <stdio.h>
6  #include <errno.h>
7  #include <stdlib.h>
8  #include <stdint.h>
9  #include <fcntl.h>
10 #include <unistd.h>
11 #include <sys/ioctl.h>
12 #include <linux/types.h>
13 #include <linux/spi/spidev.h>
14
15 static int fd = -1;
16
17 static void
18 errxit(const char *msg) {
19         perror(msg);
20         exit(1);
21 }
22
23 int
24 main(int argc, char ** argv) {
25         static uint8_t tx[] = {0x12, 0x23, 0x45, 0x67};
26         static uint8_t rx[] = {0xFF, 0xFF, 0xFF, 0xFF};
27         struct spi_ioc_transfer ioc = {
28                 .tx_buf = (unsigned long) tx,
29                 .rx_buf = (unsigned long) rx,
30                 .len = 4,
31                 .speed_hz = 100000,
32                 .delay_usecs = 10,
33                 .bits_per_word = 8,
34                 .cs_change = 1
35         } ;
36         uint8_t mode = SPI_MODE_0;
37         int rc;
38
39         fd = open("/dev/spidev0.0",O_RDWR);
40         if ( fd < 0 )
41                 errxit("Opening SPI device.");
42
```

```
43        rc = ioctl(fd,SPI_IOC_WR_MODE,&mode);
44        if ( rc < 0 )
45                errxit("ioctl (2) setting SPI mode.");
46
47        rc = ioctl(fd,
          SPI_IOC_WR_BITS_PER_WORD,
          &ioc.bits_per_word);
48        if ( rc < 0 )
49                errxit("ioctl (2) setting SPI bits perword.");
50
51        rc = ioctl(fd,SPI_IOC_MESSAGE(1),&ioc);
52        if ( rc < 0 )
53                errxit("ioctl (2) for SPI I/O");
54        close(fd);
55
56        printf("rc=%d %02X %02X %02X %02X\n",
57                rc, rx[0], rx[1], rx[2], rx[3]);
58        return 0;
59 }
```

■ ■ ■

Glossary

AC
Alternating current

Amps
Amperes

ATAG
ARM tags, though now used by boot loaders for other architectures

AVC
Advanced Video Coding (MPEG-4)

AVR
Wikipedia states that "it is commonly accepted that AVR stands for Alf (Egil Bogen) and Vegard (Wollan)'s RISC processor."

BCD
Binary-coded decimal

Brick
To accidently render a device unusable by making changes to it

CEA
Consumer Electronics Association

cond
Condition variable

CPU
Central processing unit

CRC
Cyclic redundancy check, a type of hash for error detection

CVT
Coordinated Video Timings standard (replaces GTF)

daemon
A Unix process that services requests in the background

DC
Direct current

DCD
> RS-232 data carrier detect

DCE
> RS-232 data communications equipment

Distro
> A specific distribution of Linux software

DLNA
> Digital Living Network Alliance, whose purpose is to enable sharing of digital media between multimedia devices

DMM
> Digital multimeter

DMT
> Display Monitor Timing standard

DPI
> Display Pixel Interface (a parallel display interface)

DPVL
> Digital Packet Video Link

DSI
> Display Serial Interface

DSR
> RS-232 data set ready

DTE
> RS-232 data terminal equipment

DTR
> RS-232 data terminal ready

ECC
> Error-correcting code

EDID
> Extended display identification data

EEPROM
> Electrically erasable programmable read-only memory

EMMC
> External mass media controller

Flash
> Similar to EEPROM, except that large blocks must be entirely rewritten in an update operation

FFS
> Flash file system

FIFO
First in, first out

FSP
Flash storage processor

FTL
Flash translation layer

FUSE
Filesystem in Userspace (File system in USErspace)

GNU
GNU is not Unix

GPIO
General-purpose input/output

GPU
Graphics processing unit

GTF
Generalized Timing Formula

H.264
MPEG-4 Advanced Video Coding (AVC)

H-Bridge
An electronic circuit configuration that allows voltage to be reversed across the load

HDMI
High-Definition Multimedia Interface

HID
Human interface device

I2C
Two-wire interface invented by Philips

IC
Integrated circuit

IDE
Integrated development environment

IR
Infrared

ISP
Image Sensor Pipeline

JFFS2
Journalling Flash File System 2

LCD
Liquid-crystal display

LED
Light-emitting diode

mA
Milliamperes, a measure of current flow

MCU
Microcontroller unit

MMC
MultiMedia Card

MISO
Master in, slave out

MOSI
Master out, slave in

MTD
Memory technology device

mutex
Mutually exclusive

NTSC
National Television System Committee (analog TV signal standard)

PAL
Phase Alternating Line (analog TV signal standard)

PC
Personal computer

PCB
Printed circuit board

PLL
Phase-locked loop

PoE
Power over Ethernet (supplying power over an Ethernet cable)

POSIX
Portable Operating System Interface (for Unix)

pthreads
POSIX threads

PWM
Pulse-width modulation

Pxe
Preboot execution environment, usually referencing booting by network

RAM
Random-access memory

RI
 RS-232 ring indicator

RISC
 Reduced instruction set computer

RH
 Relative humidity

ROM
 Read-only memory

RPi
 Raspberry Pi

RS-232
 Recommended standard 232 (serial communications)

RTC
 Real-time clock

SBC
 Single-board computer

SD
 Secure Digital Association memory card

SDIO
 SD card input/output interface

SDRAM
 Synchronous dynamic random-access memory

SoC
 System on a chip

SMPS
 Switched-mode power supply

SPI
 Serial Peripheral Interface (bus)

Stick parity
 Mark or space parity, where the bit is constant

TWI
 Two-wire interface

UART
 Universal asynchronous receiver/transmitter

USB
 Universal Serial Bus

V3D
 Video for 3D

VAC
Volts AC

VESA
Video Electronics Standards Association

VFS
Virtual file system

VNC
Virtual Network Computing

V_{SB}
ATX standby voltage

YAFFS
Yet Another Flash File System

■ ■ ■

Power Standards

The following table references the standard ATX power supply voltages, regulation (tolerance), and voltage ranges.[15]

The values listed here for the +5 V and +3.3 V supplies were referenced in Chapter 2 as a basis for acceptable power supply ranges. When the BroadCom power specifications become known, they should be used instead.

Supply (Volts)	Tolerance		Minimum	Maximum	Ripple (Peak to Peak)
+5 V	±5%	± 0.25 V	+4.75 V	+5.25 V	50 mV
-5 V	±10%	±0.50 V	–4.50 V	–5.50 V	50 mV
+12 V	±5%	±0.60 V	+11.40 V	+12.60 V	120 mV
-12 V	±10%	±1.2 V	–10.8 V	–13.2 V	120 mV
+3.3 V	±5%	±0.165 V	+3.135 V	+3.465 V	50 mV
+5 *VSB*	±5%	±0.25 V	+4.75 V	+5.25 V	50 mV

Electronics Reference

The experienced electronic hobbyist or engineer will already know these formulas and units well. This reference material is provided as a convenience for the student or beginning hobbiest.

Ohm's Law

Using the following triangle, cover the unknown property to determine the formula needed. For example, if current (I) is unknown, cover the I, and the formula $\dfrac{V}{R}$ remains.

Power

Power can be computed from these formulas:

$$P = I \times V$$
$$P = I^2 \times R$$
$$P = \frac{V^2}{R}$$

Units

The following chart summarizes the main metric prefixes used in electronics.

	Name	Prefix	Factor
Multiples	mega	M	10^6
	kilo	k	10^3
Fraction	milli	m	10^{-3}
	micro	μ	10^{-6}
	nano	n	10^{-9}
	pico	p	10^{-12}

Index

Get the eBook for only $10!

Now you can take the weightless companion with you anywhere, anytime. Your purchase of this book entitles you to 3 electronic versions for only $10.

This Apress title will prove so indispensible that you'll want to carry it with you everywhere, which is why we are offering the eBook in 3 formats for only $10 if you have already purchased the print book.

Convenient and fully searchable, the PDF version enables you to easily find and copy code—or perform examples by quickly toggling between instructions and applications. The MOBI format is ideal for your Kindle, while the ePUB can be utilized on a variety of mobile devices.

Go to www.apress.com/promo/tendollars to purchase your companion eBook.